THE COMPLETE ADVOCATE

A Practice File for Representing Clients from Beginning to End

THE COMPLETE ADVOCATE

A Practice File for Representing Clients from Beginning to End

A.G. Harmon, J.D., Ph.D.
The Columbus School of Law
The Catholic University of America
Washington, D.C.

Library of Congress Cataloging-in-Publication Data

Harmon, A. G., 1962-

   The complete advocate : a practice file for representing clients from beginning to end / A.G. Harmon.

    p. cm.

   ISBN 978-1-4224-2992-1 (perfect bound)

1. Practice of law—United States. 2. Attorney and client—United States. 3. Trial practice—United States. I. Title.

   KF300.H368 2010

   347.73'504—dc22

                                                 2010009320

Editorial Offices
121 Chanlon Road, New Providence, NJ 07974(908) 464-6800
201 Mission St., San Francisco, CA 94105-1831 (415) 908-3200
www.lexisnexis.com

MATTHEW◆BENDER   (2010–Pub.3291)

TABLE OF CONTENTS

ACKNOWLEDGMENTS

The author would like to thank the faculty and staff of The Columbus School of Law at The Catholic University of America for their support, particularly his colleagues Lisa Everhart, Beverly Jennison, Frederick Woods, Laurie Lewis, Olivia Farrar, and Victor Williams. He would also like to acknowledge the research assistance of Michael Willats, J.D. 2009, and the editorial assistance of Jennifer A. Beszley of LexisNexis.

INTRODUCTION

A common complaint about law school is that students are not given the big picture. They learn bits and pieces of the law—some theory, some practice, some skills—but are never quite sure how, where, or especially when, a particular piece of knowledge fits into the overall task of a client's representation. In other words, despite their education, they seldom get a bird's eye view of the entire process, from start to finish, so that they can see all of the dimensions that a legal problem might entail.

The Complete Advocate is designed to guide a student through all aspects of a legal process: researching an area of law, exhausting administrative remedies, filing pleadings, writing and arguing motions, proposing settlement, and pursuing and arguing appeals—from the beginning of the process to the end. The case file includes intake memos and assignments, for the purpose of drafting pleadings; a variety of litigation documents—depositions, affidavits, and exhibits—for the purpose of preparing litigation memoranda; motions and an order from the district court, for purposes of filing appeals; and even private, confidential facts (in the teacher's manual) for use in a mediation session. The text's purpose is not only to provide students with an education in the substantive and procedural dimensions of the subject matter, but also to provide them with a paradigm for practice—a conceptual model from which they can pattern their future approaches to a litigation matter, regardless of its type. Having "seen" and experienced the development of a case from its first step to its final resolution, students will have a fair estimation of what needs to be done throughout the course of a matter, and can gain a surer footing and orientation as to where they are when brought into the middle of an ongoing lawsuit.

This larger view of the legal landscape—from a case's inception to its conclusion—is portable knowledge that can be transferred to the nature of any particular enterprise.

The facts of the case, set in the Fifth Circuit, revolve around the Age Discrimination in Employment Act (ADEA). The primary ADEA suit involves a 57 year-old architect, Edward Morgan, suing his former employer, Architronics, Inc., a high-concept architecture firm, for replacing him with a younger, less qualified worker under the pretense of job obsolescence. The plaintiff is one of three people in a design group whose jobs were eliminated; he and another member of that group, Elizabeth Allen, 61, are in the protected class, and a third member of the group, Harris McKenna, 35, was their administrative assistant and part-time draftsman. Morgan has several theories of recovery regarding his ADEA suit. The firm contends it needed a state-of-the art computer-assisted design ("CAD") program called *Quixotic 3000* to compete professionally, and that proficiency in CAD, which the plaintiff did not possess, was demanded of all its employees. In addition, Elizabeth Allen has agreed to early retirement at this point, but the deal is not finished. Architronics has an answer to all of these claims, but the cases must be carefully argued. Administrative remedies, pleadings, discovery, motions and briefs (and attendant arguments) pertinent to trial and appellate advocacy, client correspondence and settlement negotiations—are all dimensions of the text, ordered so that students may gain the full perspective of the advocate. In addition, assignments are written from the perspective of one of the law firms representing the parties: Hopkins, Eliot, and Jones (Plaintiff) and Conrad and Conrad (Defendant).

The chief advantage of the multi-dimensional approach of this book is that it can be used to teach a variety of skills involving the same fact situation. A professor may custom design the focus of the class in terms of the substantive area, the scope of the research, and the types of assignments chosen. Versatility is a hallmark.

Dates

To prevent the text from becoming out of date, dates are set out according to the following key:

The current year = YEAR (e.g., January 1, YEAR)

A year before the current year = YR-1 (e.g. January 1, YR-1)

Two years before the current year = YR-2 (e.g. January 1, YR-2)

A year *from* the current year = YR+1 (January 1, YR+1)

Two years *from* the current year = YR+2 (e.g. January 1, YR+2); etc., etc.

Pagination

The book is paginated consecutively at the bottom of each page; however, documents for use in the two appellate brief/argument assignments—Assignments 6 and 10 are also paginated in the top right corner, so that they can be assembled with other court documents to provide a record on appeal. The Complaint and Answer for each of the two appellate problems are included in the Teacher's Manual, in the event the professor would like to assign pleadings drafting exercises—Assignments # 5 and #9. When the appellate record is assembled, it should accord with the pagination at the beginning of the Complaint, top right corner, and proceed in order as the documents dictate. References to the record in each of the two Bench Briefs relate to this pagination scheme.

MORGAN V. ARCHITRONICS, INC.: PARTIES/PRINCIPALS

Stephen Abernathy, Vice President, Architronics, Inc.

Elizabeth Allen, 61, architect at Architronics, Inc.; colleague of Edward Morgan.

Ellen Ambrose, real estate paralegal, Victoria office, Hopkins, Eliot and Jones.

Architronics, Inc., Defendant, represented by Hopkins, Eliot, and Jones.

Henry C. Baker, 49, President and owner, Architronics, Inc.

Madeleine Cason, legal secretary to G. Mark Hopkins, Hopkins, Eliot and Jones.

Rebecca A. Conrad, Conrad and Conrad, LLP, lead counsel for Plaintiff.

John Eliot, senior partner, Hopkins, Eliot and Jones.

Margaret Ellison, 49, CAD Specialist, Architronics, Inc.

Jane Fletcher, Senior Vice President and head of Victoria office, Architronics, Inc.

Charlotte Davidson, Office Manager, Architronics, Inc.

Katherine Granbury, Administrative Assistant, Architronics, Inc.

G. Mark Hopkins, managing partner, Hopkins, Eliot and Jones; lead counsel for Defendant.

Virginia Latham, supervising attorney, Victoria office, Hopkins, Eliot and Jones.

Harris McKenna, 35, Administrative Assistant to Morgan and Allen.

Edward J. Morgan, 57, Plaintiff, Design Specialist, Architronics, Inc., represented by Conrad & Conrad, LLP.

Robinson and Porter Attorneys, Victoria, Texas, former employers of Ellen Ambrose.

Philip Whitlow, CFO, Architronics, Inc.

Assignment 1

ADMINISTRATIVE REMEDIES

Hopkins, Eliot, and Jones
Attorneys at Law
567 Harrison Place South
Corpus Christi, Texas 78470
Telephone: 316-555-4312
Facsimile: 316-555-2111
hejlawfirm.com

INTEROFFICE MEMORANDUM

From: G. Mark Hopkins
To: Drafting Attorney
Re: Architronics/Elizabeth Allen Matter
Date: Today, YEAR.

Having met yesterday with Henry Baker, Jr. president of our client, Architronics, Inc., the following facts relate to a matter involving the company and one of its former employees, Elizabeth Allen.

Three weeks ago, Elizabeth Allen, a 61 year-old architect with the Corpus Christi architecture firm, Architronics, Inc., was approached by the president of the company, Henry Baker. Baker explained that the company was in trouble, owing to a variety of reasons, but particularly due to its loss of business. Achitronics' competitors were utilizing the latest computer-assisted design (CAD) software, *Quixotic 3000*, a program that provided state-of-the art presentations that also cut costs for the customer. Architronics had foregone the purchase of Quixotic and was now paying the price in lost projects.

As a result, Baker explained, the only measure the company felt it could take was to reduce its force in the main branch of the firm in Corpus Christi. Allen's position, as well as that of her fellow architect and job boss, Edward Morgan, 57, and that of their administrative assistant, Harris McKenna, 35, was to be eliminated. The three formed a Design Group that was, in Architronics view, the least proficient in CAD. Allen was given an option. She could take a position at a satellite office of the firm, in Victoria, Texas—about seventy-five miles away. The new job was basically at the same salary and retained the same benefits, but it was as an Assistant Design Specialist and she would have no expense account. As an alternative, Allen could take early retirement, which she was not eligible to receive for another year, when she turned 62. She was told that she had three days to consider her choice, but as time was of the essence for the company, they needed a decision at the end of that time. The offer of a job in Victoria was also made later that day to Edward Morgan. The meeting took place Friday morning. Allen, somewhat flustered, decided not to wait. She agreed to the early retirement before she left the office that day.

Allen has been employed with Architronics for ten years. Her current annual salary is $110,000/year, plus remuneration for professional advancement, conferences, and continuing education. Her early retirement offer consists of a severance portion and a pension. The severance

4

portion is two weeks of pay per year on the job, calculated at her annual salary rate at the time of termination. All salaried employees with the firm receive severance under this formula if the circumstances of their departure involve retirement or job elimination (but not for those who are terminated for cause).

Absent the early retirement offer, Allen would be eligible to retire with full pension benefits at the age of 62. Architronics' standard pension formula is an employee's years of service *times* 1.5% of her annual salary at the time of retirement. Thus, if Allen had been eligible for retirement this year, her annual pension would have been $16,500 (10 × (1.5% of $110,000)). Under the terms of the early retirement offer, her pension is calculated as if she were 62 and had worked for 11 years. In addition, for pension calculation purposes, her annual salary at the time of the buyout is deemed to be $113,300, reflecting a 3% cost of living adjustment. Thus, her annual pension in the first year of the buyout is $18,695 (rounded up to the nearest dollar). Beginning on January 1, YR+2 and in each successive year, her annual pension will be increased by a percentage amount pegged to the Bureau of Labor Statistics Consumer Price Index for Urban Wage Earners and Clerical Workers (CPI-W), U.S. City Average, All Items, 1982–84 = 100. The rate of increase will be equal to 60% of the percentage change between the average CPI for the calendar year in which she retired and the average CPI for the 12-month period ending August 31 immediately preceding the year when the adjustment is payable. Unless she signs the waiver, company reimbursement of her membership fees in several professional organizations and her registration fees at two premier, yearly design conferences will be discontinued.

Baker knows that Elizabeth Allen has talked with Edward Morgan, her former colleague. Baker says that Morgan has obtained an attorney to pursue an age discrimination suit under the Age Discrimination in Employment Act (ADEA). Morgan claims that he and Allen were the targets of ageist comments, and that the *Quixotic*/lagging business excuse is a pretext. In his opinion, the job offer in Victoria amounted to constructive discharge, as the drive was impossible for him, due to family considerations of which Architronics is well aware. He will likely not sign a waiver. Harris McKenna, Allen and Morgan's administrative assistant, is also considering suit on independent grounds, but he is only 35.

At this point, Allen has not signaled any intentions different from those of three weeks ago, when she agreed to early retirement. After she accepted Architronics offer on the day it was made, Allen went to one of the aforementioned conferences, in Germany, with all expenses paid by the company. She is to return next week and is scheduled to meet with Baker next Thursday. At that meeting, Architronics wants to seize the moment and obtain her waiver of any ADEA claim she might have against the company. Below are some of the things that the company would like communicated to Allen as part of the waiver's terms:

1. Architronics will continue to pay Allen's membership fees and registration fees for the next four years (until she reaches age 65; her birthday is April 14th) if she signs the waiver.

2. Severance will be payable in a lump sum upon Allen's execution of the Agreement.
3. Upon execution of the Agreement, Allen will be entitled to begin receiving her annual pension, payable in roughly equal monthly installments, by direct deposit on the first day of each month to a bank Allen designates.
4. Any consideration paid to Allen in exchange for the waiver will have to be returned if she reneges and decides to sue under the ADEA.
5. Keeping any portion of the consideration after a suit is filed will be tantamount to the waiver's ratification.
6. Any recovery under an ADEA suit would be subject to set-off against payments received in consideration of the wavier.
7. Architronics' attorney's fees incurred in any ADEA suit brought by Allen would be recoverable.
8. Allen will not communicate with Morgan, McKenna, or any third party with regard to the reduction in force.
9. Architronics would like for the waiver to be effective upon signing.

I also have some questions about the procedure of enforcing such a waiver, which you should answer in an accompanying memo.

1. If she were to challenge this waiver, how will the burdens of proof run in a lawsuit?
2. Allen is very talented and Architronics wants to have her sign a covenant not to compete, effective until she turns 65. It would like to allocate portions of the severance and retirement package as consideration in return for a separate covenant not to compete. Would such an allocation benefit the company if the court finds her ADEA waiver to be invalid for some reason? At present, do not yet draft the covenant not to compete.
3. At some point after we deliver the waiver, Allen may come back with a counter-offer, wanting more money, more perks, etc. If we agree to amend a certain provision in our offer, will doing so have any effect on the waiver's enforceability?
4. What kind of records/information should Architronics keep and how will it need to conduct itself in the event of an Equal Employment Opportunity Commission (EEOC) investigation? I've appended a statement today from Architronics' office manager as to what they do, but is it sufficient as far as the regulations are concerned?

Prior to drafting, please read the United States Supreme Court decision in *Oubre v. Entergy Operations, Inc.*, 522 U.S. 422 (1998). The text of the Older Workers Benefit Protection Act (OWBPA), which I believe amends the ADEA in some fashion, is appended to the opinion of the court. It should be updated to make sure that it has not been changed since the case was handed down. Also consult the applicable EEOC regulations,

29 C.F.R. §§ 1625.22, 1625.23 (2008). Then draft the waiver so that it accords with the pertinent law, and also accompany it with the above-referenced memo, explaining any potential problems or difficulties in the approach Architronics has requested.

GMH:mc

Attachments

Architronics, Inc.
9876 Upper Broadway Street
Corpus Christi, Texas 78401

Today, YEAR

G. Mark Hopkins, Esq.
Hopkins, Eliot, and Jones
Attorneys at Law
567 Harrison Place South
Corpus Christi, Texas 78470
Re: Employee Data
Mr. Hopkins,

It is my understanding that an EEOC action might be filed against our company by up to two former employees. At your request, I met with our human resources officer and reviewed the company's current protocols with regard to employee records.

At present, the Human Resources Department has on file:

1. All employee evaluations, current and former.
2. All job descriptions and changes made thereto with regard to all current employment positions and those that are no longer part of Architronics' business structure.
3. Continuing Education compliance for each employee, current and former.
4. Any formal, employment-related complaints made against employees and any formal, employment-related reprimands against employees, whether made by management or by myself as Office Manager. This data is kept in this office for two years.

I have also spoken with our CFO, Philip Whitlow, who can provide us with records as to payroll, pay scales, bonuses, benefit plans, and expenditures for the past three years.

We have not had an EEOC charge filed against the company before, so the format of this documentation may not be in the proper form. At this point, I haven't been told whether any particular employee(s) data should be amassed. Please advise me on those issues. Finally, if there is other information we should gather (other than that outlined above), regarding particular issues that are the subject of the charge(s), please advise me on how to proceed.

Sincerely,

Charlotte Davidson
Charlotte Davidson,
Office Manager
Architronics, Inc.

Conrad & Conrad, LLP
Suite 1056, Commerce Place
Corpus Christi, Texas 78470
Telephone: 316-555-2134
Facsimile: 316-555-1211
conrad@conrad.com

INTEROFFICE MEMORANDUM

From: Rebecca A. Conrad
To: Drafting Attorney
Re: Edward Morgan Matter
Date: Today, YEAR.

   As you know, Edward Morgan has retained our firm to represent him in his age discrimination suit against his former employer, Architronics, Inc. Attached is the basic information received from him in the initial client interview. In a memorandum, explain:

1) what information we will need to initiate this action with the Equal Employment Opportunity (EEOC);
2) how a charge is filed with the EEOC;
3) who notifies the employer of the charge;
4) how a claim is made under the Texas state age discrimination law (and what effect that the two claims, under state and federal law, have on each other);
5) how a private action for age discrimination is maintained, and what happens if the EEOC dismisses the charge.

Prepare all necessary documents to initiate the administrative remedies.

Rac/bb

Attachment

Assignment 2

CLOSED UNIVERSE MEMORANDUM

From: Senior Attorney, Corpus Christi, Texas Law Firm
To: Junior Associate
Date: Today, YEAR
Re: Katherine Granbury

Yesterday, I met with Katherine Granbury of New Orleans, Louisiana. She moved here with her husband, a naval officer stationed out of New Orleans, but reassigned for a period of time to the Corpus Christi Naval Air Station. The couple knew they would be here in Texas for a period of anywhere between eighteen and thirty-six months. As they planned to return to Louisiana afterwards, they rented out their house there. Ms. Granbury did not change her place of residence.

Ms. Granbury is a former employee of Architronics, Inc., an architecture firm here. Granbury was hired on March 16, YR-1, and has since that time been employed as an administrative assistant. There was no time limit stated for her employment status, only an agreed upon wage per hour payment for prescribed duties.

There was no written contract between Architronics and Ms. Granbury, but her supervisor, Charlotte Davidson, the office manager, provided her with an employee handbook upon the first day of her employ. No action on the part of the employee was called for by the company with regard to the distributed handbook. The beginning of the handbook includes a section entitled "Statement of Purpose." It says that the rules provided therein are meant simply to guide the employees in employment matters.

The handbook was distributed to all employees by Ms. Davidson. In addition, according to Ms. Granbury, Ms. Davidson constantly referred employees to their "contract" with the company, meaning the handbook, when employment questions came up about procedural matters such as vacation time, office parties, use of company services for personal matters, and rights regarding worker's compensation.

Handbook provision III.A.5 states that an employee may be terminated at any time, but only for good cause. The handbook lists several reasons for termination:

Termination for Good Cause includes the following:
1) **Failure to log in and out of billing system: Because billing of clients is determined at an hourly rate, it is crucial that all employees log in and out of their computer systems consistently. Repeated failures of this type will result in termination. Any difficulty operating the system, or any malfunction of the system, must be brought to the supervisor's attention immediately....**

The next section of the handbook, III.A.6, says that in the event of an employee' termination for one of the things in the enumerated list:

[T]he personnel committee, consisting of three firm partners, can review the office manager's decision to terminate for good cause upon the employee's request. The request

12

must be made within ten days of the decision to terminate. The committee's review, once undertaken, must give its decision to the employee within a week of its meeting.

In her yearly evaluation, Ms. Granbury was cited for failing to log in and out of her computer. She states that this was only one instance, and also states that a fellow employee was terminated a year ago only after ten such instances.

During the first full week of August, YEAR, Ms. Granbury was ill. Upon returning to work, she was met with a new log-in/log-out procedure, installed in her absence. As it turned out, the system was not operating properly, and two weeks worth of billing was lost. Ms. Granbury was unaware of the system's malfunction. She was discharged according to handbook provision III.A.5. on August 13, YEAR. She made a request for review by the personnel committee within a week, but the committee did not take up the request. To her certain knowledge, which she can corroborate with testimony by employees that have worked at the firm since its inception, the committee has never refused to take up a request to consider termination, including that of the employee dismissed a year ago for ten billing procedure infractions.

This incident has had many financial and emotional ramifications for Ms. Granbury and her family. I'm aware of the case attached, *Aiello v. United Air Lines, Inc.*, 818 F.2d 1196 (5th Cir. 1987), and need a quick response to whether Ms. Granbury has a claim regarding her discharge under what began as an "at-will" employment relationship between her and Architronics. Draft a memo to answer this question. At this point, focus only on whether the relationship between Ms. Granbury and her former employer was changed by the circumstances (not on whether the cause was a "good" one or not).

Limit your use of authority to this one case, and assume we'll keep our options open as to when to file, where to file, and what precisely to ask for by way of remedy (though I can foresee monetary damages, costs, penalties, etc. in the range of $100,000).

OPEN UNIVERSE MEMORANDUM

Conrad & Conrad, LLP
Suite 1056, Commerce Place
Corpus Christi, Texas 78470
Telephone: 316-555-2134
Facsimile: 316-555-1211
conrad@conrad.com

To: New Associate
From: Rebecca Conrad
Re: Edward Morgan—Retaliatory Discharge Claim (Client # 024-32)
Date: Today, YEAR

Today, I met with Edward Morgan regarding what he believes to be acts of retribution taken against him by his employer, Architronics, Inc., an upscale architecture firm here in Corpus Christi, Texas. Mr. Morgan, 57, has been a longtime employee there, working as a Design Specialist. He has had some disagreements with management over the past year or so.

Mr. Morgan wants to know if he can seek redress against his employer for age discrimination under the federal Age Discrimination in Employment Act (ADEA). That claim, which we would file in federal court here in the Southern District of Texas, is rather involved, requiring the plaintiff to establish a prima facie case for employer misconduct of a proscribed nature, followed by a burden shifting analysis.

At this point, however, as we are simply trying to determine whether Mr. Morgan can establish a prima facie case of employer misconduct, I would like you to research and explain whether the facts in the attached file will support a valid complaint for retaliatory discharge. Therefore, I am not yet interested in the burden shifting requirements that follow the establishment of the employer misconduct. I am also not yet interested in any state law claims that Mr. Morgan might have.

Provide me with a memo on this matter.

RAC/jj

1 Ms. Conrad: This is a client interview with Edward Morgan, at our down-
2 town offices of Conrad and Conrad, LLP, in Corpus Christi. The date is
3 TODAY, YEAR. It's 10:30 A.M. Present are myself, Rebecca Conrad—
4 Mr. Morgan, our client—and the firm stenographer, Cecilia Miller.
5
6 Q: Mr. Morgan, would you state your full name, age, and address?
7
8 A: Edward James Morgan, 57. I live at 5678 Church Street, Kingsville,
9   Texas.
10
11 Q: And Kingsville is how far from Corpus Christi?
12
13 A: About twenty miles southwest of town.
14
15 Q: And where are you employed?
16
17 A: Well, I'm on leave right now—I'm taking an extended vacation of two
18   weeks—from Architronics, Inc.
19
20 Q: That's an architecture firm here in town, correct?
21
22 A: Yes.
23
24 Q: And what's your occupation at Architronics?
25
26 A: I'm a Design Specialist. That's a type of architect.
27
28 Q: What's your background in that field?
29
30 A: I received a B.A. degree from Texas Tech in YR-37. I worked for a
31   local firm for five or six years before I moved to Dallas and started
32   a partnership with a school friend for ten years. Then I moved back
33   home, as my wife wanted to come back to be close to her family. I'd
34   worked with the founder of this company as a colleague for years—not
35   Mr. Baker—his predecessor, Mr. Williams—and he asked me to join
36   his group, Architronics, in YR-11.
37
38 Q: How big is the firm? I mean, how many architects?
39
40 A: I believe—let's see—about twenty-four—yes twenty-four here at the
41   main office, and another six in the branch we have in Victoria, Texas.
42
43 Q: Are there different types of architects in a firm that size?
44
45 A: Yes, there're staff architects, and then above them, the project managers,
46   who keep things on time and within budget. They're on the same level

47		with both the senior designers, who decide the look of the project, and
48		the job captains, who ensure the functionality of the work—that is,
49		that it actually does what it's designed to do. Above everyone are the
50		principal architects, who sign off on the whole thing. The president of
51		the company, Henry Baker, is a principal architect.
52		
53	Q:	And what kind of architect is a Design specialist within that
54		hierarchy?
55		
56	A:	I have a special role, as a senior draftsman, which is a kind of Design
57		Specialist. I draw construction details and make sure that the designs
58		are functional—in other words, the building actually stands up, heats
59		and cools, can withstand the elements—that kind of thing. I also have
60		job captain responsibilities.
61		
62	Q:	So tell me about the events that led to your problems with your
63		employer.
64		
65	A:	All right. I guess, if I had to say, it all began last January. It may
66		have been brewing for a time before that, come to think of it. But last
67		January was when it came to a head.
68		
69	Q:	What do you mean precisely? What came to a head?
70		
71	A:	Well, as I explained, I'm a senior draftsman with years and years of
72		experience. For the most part, that experience had been respected by
73		the firm up until recently.
74		
75	Q:	Things changed?
76		
77	A:	They did. About a year ago, there was this big push by the firm to
78		modify the image. We've always been a high-concept architecture firm,
79		dealing with the latest in design for special customers like museums,
80		upscale restaurants, civic showpieces—planetariums and amphithe-
81		aters—the kind of buildings that show up in brochures about an area.
82		I've been as proud of that as anyone there. But about a year ago, there
83		was a push to stress the kinds of presentations we made—the kinds of
84		"pitches" that we sold to clients—so that they were the "latest thing."
85		More and more, the CAD work we'd—"
86		
87	Q:	Excuse me. Explain that. What's "CAD"?
88		
89	A:	Oh. "Computer-Assisted Design." Basically, it's architecture done
90		with computer programs. They've been around a while. There've been
91		advancements in technical fields like ours, just as there have been in
92		other fields, and we've kept up with that. We use those programs, to
93		the extent they're helpful.

94	Q:	All right. Go ahead. You were saying about the CAD work?
95		
96	A:	Well, more and more, there was this big push from the company's lead-
97		ership to employ CAD work in every dimension of what we were doing.
98		I make pitches to clients myself. But that job can be done well with
99		the kind of high-quality draftsmanship that I do. Don't get me wrong.
100		I'm not opposed to CAD work. I just don't think that it should take
101		preeminence. It's not a substitute for the integrity of the project, which
102		can be assured by the basic principals of good architecture—and mak-
103		ing presentations exclusively in CAD is just wrong-headed. That's my
104		view. That's what I expressed. And that's what apparently antagonized
105		some people—or rather, that's what brought out the truth regarding
106		how they feel about me.
107		
108	Q:	What do you mean? Who are you referring to?
109		
110	A:	Well, Stephen Abernathy, one of the vice presidents, was the biggest
111		cheerleader for this new "CAD vision" thing, as I call it. He pushed
112		hard for us to be as high-tech as possible, in the way we practiced our
113		field and in the way we presented ourselves to the public. I mean, he
114		wanted us to be cutting edge in every aspect—to be known for that.
115		I brought in a clipping from the newspaper about it. Some interview
116		he gave last summer. It gives you an idea how crazy he is for this stuff,
117		which is one reason the firm has had problems, if you ask me. There
118		have been rumors around that we aren't doing as good as we might be,
119		financially—we've lost some bids—and all of this seemed like a rush to
120		fix things in the wrong way. I objected and told him so. I didn't think
121		we ought to reinvent ourselves in such a way.
122		
123	Q:	When did you say all this?
124		
125	A:	I guess—as I said—it was in January of this year. He came by my office
126		and asked to talk. He said that he'd heard I was putting up some resis-
127		tance to this new vision for the company. I asked him where he'd heard
128		that, and he shrugged and said Philip Whitlow had told him.
129		
130	Q:	Who's he? "Whitlow"?
131		
132	A:	The Chief Financial Officer. They're big friends, he and Abernathy;
133		lunch together all the time. Whitlow had told Abernathy about a conver-
134		sation at a staff meeting we'd had—one where everybody was clamber-
135		ing to get this new software Abernathy had been pushing. Everybody
136		but me and my colleague, Elizabeth Allen—who's older than I am, by
137		the way. We said we thought it was a bad idea, to overhaul ourselves
138		like this. I said that presentations using CAD would just be a sell-out to
139		faddishness; I said people ought to listen to me, as I'd been around a lot
140		longer than anybody who thought this was a good idea. So apparently

141		Abernathy got word of this from Whitlow, and he came into my office
142		that day wanting know about what I'd said. I just told him flat out that
143		it was true. That's the way I felt—that's the way I feel still.
144		
145	Q:	What did Mr. Abernathy say then?
146		
147	A:	He said that was an "old way" of thinking. He said that all the young
148		people in the firm understood this vision and I had to get up to date.
149		Then I said I didn't exactly like the way he put that. I said he was turn-
150		ing this into a boutique firm full of computer jockeys. And then he got
151		all red in the face and said how the firm was run and what direction
152		it was to take was for management to decide, not somebody who was
153		there when they invented protractors. Well, of course, that got me mad,
154		and I told him he didn't have a right to talk to me like that—I said
155		that I knew my rights—and that, even "old" as I was, I wouldn't take
156		that lying down. I've had to put up with Whitlow and others calling me
157		"Leonardo da Vinci" and stuff—like that was funny. I knew what they
158		meant. Once, he even called me that around Henry—Baker, I mean,
159		the president of the company—and they kind of smiled together.
160		
161	Q:	What happened next?
162		
163	A:	He left, mad. And I sat there, mad. It took a week or two for me to cool
164		down. I talked some around the office about getting in touch with a law-
165		yer, about the way I was being treated. I looked into my rights under
166		the age discrimination laws too. I ordered some government pamphlets
167		and set them out around the break room and in the lobby, as a kind of
168		protest. Whitlow saw me. But it all passed over.
169		
170	Q:	You haven't spoken with Mr. Abernathy since?
171		
172	A:	We ignored each other. But we spoke in meetings after a while. In time,
173		we seemed to have this mutual, unspoken agreement to play like it had
174		never occurred.
175		
176	Q:	Go ahead. What happened then, after January?
177		
178	A:	Nothing with regards to me and Abernathy. But in August—August 2
179		to be precise—Henry Baker, the president of the firm, wanted to see
180		me just as I was coming back to the office from a business call. He let
181		me know that because of the financial straits the firm was in, they'd
182		decided to reduce the force in our office here. He said there were some
183		Assistant Design Specialist positions in the Victoria office, though,
184		which he was offering me and Elizabeth.
185		
186	Q:	Victoria is—what?—about an hour and half north of Corpus Christi?
187		
188	A:	Yes. And the job was as an Assistant Design Specialist, not a Design
189		Specialist. It did carry just about the same salary and all the same

190		benefits, but the title would be different and I'd lose my expense
191		account. And that commute would be hard on me—considering that
192		I already live south of here.
193		
194	Q:	Did you think of relocating?
195		
196	A:	I can't. I have a daughter whose husband died last year and my wife
197		and I help take care of her son. Besides, Kingsville is my hometown.
198		Why should I have to relocate? At any rate, I was flabbergasted. I told
199		him I was going to take a break immediately, but that I didn't like this
200		one bit and that I thought I knew why it was happening.
201		
202	Q:	So just to be clear, you're saying that the incident back in January is
203		related to this decision two weeks ago?
204		
205	A:	Yes.
206		
207	Q:	All right, just a few more things for now. Are you proficient in CAD,
208		Mr. Morgan?
209		
210	A:	I can do it. As I said, I use an older CAD program some. I'm proficient
211		in it. Not in all the latest things, like the rest of them tend to be.
212		But as I said—architecture is more than video games.
213		
214	Q:	Can Whitlow or Abernathy discharge or reprimand employees?
215		
216	A:	No. Baker has sole hiring and firing authority.
217		
218	Q:	And you said you have a copy of an email Mr. Baker sent after the
219		meeting in which he broke the news?
220		
221	A:	Yes. I'll give it to you.
222		
223		Ms Conrad: Thank you. End of interview. 11:00 A.M.

From: Henry C. Baker [hcb@architronics.com]
Sent: August 4, YEAR
To: Morgan, Edward J.
Subject: Our talk the other day

Ed:

As I said the other day, I reviewed Philip's recommendation that we need
to shift some of our current resources to Victoria. As you know, we've done
this before. Two years ago, Martha Beauchamp and Anthony DeBertolet
moved to Victoria at our request, and it's part of our standard employment relationship that relocation to the branch office is an agreed upon
possibility, one to be acquiesced to as need requires. Together with Philip's
recommendation, and with what I know of you personally, I believe this is
the right action to take.

Sincerely,
hcb

Henry Carrington Baker, Jr.
President
Architronics, Inc.
9876 Upper Broadway Street
Corpus Christi, Texas 78401

Corpus Christi Daily Register

July 1, YEAR

Business Section (page B 1)

Image is Everything

by Ashley McKnight (Staff Reporter)

Architronics, Inc., a well-established architecture firm with offices in Corpus Christi and Victoria, with clients throughout the South and Southwest, has instituted a campaign to reassert itself in the public sphere. That plan began last fall, with a new façade that modernized their downtown headquarters. It continues today with a renewed emphasis on the kind of advanced computer-assisted designs that one of Architronics' principals believes is what the modern customer wants.

Stephen Abernathy, Senior V.P., said yesterday in a phone interview that the firm plans to make a cutting-edge statement in the world of architecture, both in the contributions it makes to skylines as well as in the way that it does its business.

"We've always stayed ahead of trends in our plans," said Abernathy. "That's evident in the kinds of projects we undertake and in the kinds of clients that seek our expertise. We're known for bringing the latest in continental design styles to the Southwest, but we want the public to know that in the future, everything about us—from the way we pitch deals, to the way we advance projects, to the way we communicate concepts, will be conducted in the latest medium possible. We're going to keep our firm perpetually young."

Recent projects have included the prized Jericho Plaza Arts Complex in Houston, the Dorothy Pollard Children's Museum in San Antonio, and the renovation of the Trifecta Planetarium in Dallas.

"Today is already too old for us," remarked Abernathy, who says everyone in the firm is of the same mind in this mission. "Tomorrow is even a little out of date."

Assignment 4

CLIENT LETTERS

Conrad & Conrad, LLP
Suite 1056, Commerce Place
Corpus Christi, Texas 78470
Telephone: 316-555-2134
Facsimile: 316-555-1211
conrad@conrad.com

INTEROFFICE MEMORANDUM

From: Rebecca A. Conrad
To: Drafting Attorney
Re: Edward Morgan Matter
Date: Today, YEAR.

Draft a client letter to Edward J. Morgan apprising him of his position with regard to a potential retaliatory discharge claim against his former employer, Architronics, Inc.

When suggesting a course of action for Mr. Morgan to take, consider the client's position under the law as you have related it to me in your interoffice memorandum on the matter.

Rac/bb

Hopkins, Eliot, and Jones
Attorneys at Law
567 Harrison Place South
Corpus Christi, Texas 78470
Telephone: 316-555-4312
Facsimile: 316-555-2111
hejlawfirm.com

INTEROFFICE MEMORANDUM

From: G. Mark Hopkins
To: Drafting Attorney
Re: Architronics Matter
Date: Today, YEAR.

Draft a client letter to Henry C. Baker, Jr., president of Architronics, Inc., apprising him of the company's position with regard to a potential retaliatory discharge claim brought by Architronics' former employee, Edward J. Morgan.

When suggesting a course of action for Architronics to take, consider the client's position under the law as you have related it to me in your interoffice memorandum on the matter.

GMH: mc

Assignment 5

PLEADINGS: ADEA

Conrad & Conrad, LLP
Suite 1056, Commerce Place
Corpus Christi, Texas 78470
Telephone: 316-555-2134
Facsimile: 316-555-1211
conrad@conrad.com

INTEROFFICE MEMORANDUM

From: Rebecca A. Conrad
To: Associate
        Today, YEAR.
Re: Edward J. Morgan

To refresh your memory about our client with regard to the matter described below, Edward J. Morgan is a fifty-seven year-old resident of 5678 Church Street, Kingsville, Texas 78363, in Kleberg County, Texas. He is a former employee of Architronics, Inc., a Texas Corporation with offices in Corpus Christi and Victoria, Texas.

Architronics, Inc. specializes in high concept architectural designs. It employs thirty-five employees in two branches: a main branch in Corpus Christi, and the other in nearby Victoria.

For ten years, Morgan had held the position of Design Specialist, the job description of which included technical drafting for building designs and meeting with clients.

On August 2, YR-1, Morgan returned from a day-long meeting with a client and was called into the office of company president, Henry Baker. Baker informed Morgan that the company had to make some immediate changes. He said that, as Morgan knew, Architronics had been in financial straits of late. The last quarter showed that the situation had grown dire. Their ability to compete with two competitors in their local markets was being eclipsed by their lack of computer-assisted design (CAD) capabilities. Specifically, a particular computer program—*Quixotic 3000*—key to servicing clients' design needs cost-effectively, was possessed by their competitors and had been determined as directly responsible for Architronics' loss of business. The program would have to be bought and implemented immediately—within the next month or two—if the company were to survive. Morgan was informed that though this was a decision no one wanted to make, Architronics had decided it was necessary to hire someone already proficient in *Quixotic*. As a result, a reduction in force was in order, and the positions possessed by Morgan and his immediate group of co-workers, Elizabeth Allen, 61, and Harris McKenna, 35, would be eliminated. The new position would replace these three.

Earlier in the day, Allen had been offered early retirement, which she had decided to take. McKenna had been let go. Morgan was offered the opportunity to work in Victoria at the same basic salary and benefits, though as an Assistant Design Specialist with a reduced expense account. Victoria is approximately seventy-five miles from Corpus Christi. Because

30

of the exigency of the circumstances, the job offer in Victoria had to be accepted in three days.

Morgan decided against the offer. The daily commute would be too long, he and his wife did not want to move from their hometown (for personal reasons), and he considered the job a demotion. He was also surprised by the news, as to his knowledge there had been no indication that a reduction in force was going to be implemented. There were rumors of hard times, but nothing as drastic as this. He has since learned that the replacement worker, Margaret Ellison, is a forty-nine year-old woman, proficient in *Quixotic 3000*, and certified to train others in its use. Morgan had never refused any training that he was asked to undergo, though he had resisted some changes as he did not think they were good business decisions by his superiors. His job evaluations prior to the news had been good, though the last set of evaluations had changed to include questions about proficiency in computer skills.

Morgan wants to know if he has a case for federal (not state) age discrimination. Draft the complaint, assuming we'll file in the Southern District of Texas.

Hopkins, Eliot, and Jones
Attorneys at Law
567 Harrison Place South
Corpus Christi, Texas 78470
Telephone: 316-555-4312
Facsimile: 316-555-2111
hejlawfirm.com

INTEROFFICE MEMORANDUM

From: G. Mark Hopkins
To: Associate
Re: Architronics, Inc.
Date: Today, YEAR.

To refresh your memory about our client with regard to the matter described below, Architronics, Inc., is a Texas Corporation with offices in Corpus Christi and Victoria, Texas. Edward J. Morgan is a fifty-seven year-old resident of 5678 Church Street, Kingsville, Texas 78363, in Kleberg County, Texas. He is a former employee of Architronics.

Architronics, Inc. specializes in high concept architectural designs. It employs thirty-five employees in its two branches. Its main branch is in Corpus Christi, and the other is in nearby Victoria.

For ten years, Morgan had held the position of Design Specialist, the job description of which included technical drafting for building designs and meeting with clients.

On August 2, YR-1, Morgan returned from a day-long meeting with a client and was called into the office of company president, Henry Baker. Baker informed Morgan that the company had to make some immediate changes. He said that, as Morgan knew, Architronics had been in financial straits of late. The last quarter showed that the situation had grown dire. Their ability to compete with two competitors in their local markets was being eclipsed by their lack of computer-assisted design (CAD) capabilities. Specifically, a particular computer program—*Quixotic 3000*—key to servicing clients' design needs cost-effectively, was possessed by their competitors and had been determined as directly responsible for Architronics' loss of business. The program would have to be bought and implemented immediately—within the next month or two—if the company were to survive. Morgan was informed that though this was a decision no one wanted to make, Architronics had decided it was necessary to hire someone already proficient in *Quixotic*. As a result, a reduction in force was in order, and the positions possessed by Morgan and his immediate group of co-workers, Elizabeth Allen, 61, and Harris McKenna, 35, would be eliminated. The new position would replace these three.

Earlier in the day, Allen had been offered early retirement, which she had decided to take. McKenna had been let go. Morgan was offered the opportunity to work in Victoria at the same basic salary and benefits, though as an Assistant Design Specialist with a reduced expense account.

Victoria is approximately seventy-five miles from Corpus Christi. Because of the exigency of the circumstances, the job offer in Victoria had to be accepted in three days.

Morgan decided against the offer. He said the daily commute would be too long, he and his wife did not want to move from their hometown (for personal reasons), and he considered the job a demotion. Since Morgan quit, the company has hired Margaret Ellison, a forty-nine year-old woman proficient in *Quixotic 3000*, and certified to train others in its use. Although Morgan had never refused any training that he was asked to undergo, he had resisted some changes as he did not think they were good business decisions by his superiors. His job evaluations prior to the news had been good, though the last set of evaluations had changed to include questions about proficiency in computer skills.

Morgan has filed a complaint for federal (not state) age discrimination, which is attached. Draft an answer to this complaint.

BRIEF: ADEA CLAIM

Hopkins, Eliot, and Jones
Attorneys at Law
567 Harrison Place South
Corpus Christi, Texas 78470
Telephone: 316-555-4312
Facsimile: 316-555-2111
hejlawfirm.com

INTEROFFICE MEMORANDUM

From: G. Mark Hopkins
To: Associate
Date: Today, YEAR
Re: Edward J. Morgan, ADEA Claim v. Architronics, Inc.

As you are aware, Architronics, Inc. in the above-styled case has filed a Motion for Summary Judgment. Edward J. Morgan intends to file a Response to that Motion.

Please draft a memorandum of law in support of the Motion for Summary Judgment.

Conrad & Conrad, LLP
Suite 1056, Commerce Place
Corpus Christi, Texas 78470
Telephone: 316-555-2134
Facsimile: 316-555-1211
conrad@conrad.com

INTEROFFICE MEMORANDUM

From: Rebecca A. Conrad
To: Associate
Date: Today, YEAR
Re: Edward J. Morgan ADEA Claim v. Architronics, Inc.

As you are aware, Architronics, Inc. in the above-styled case has filed a Motion for Summary Judgment. Edward J. Morgan intends to file a Response to that Motion.

Please draft a memorandum of law in opposition to the Motion for Summary Judgment.

1	Deposition of Henry C. Baker, Jr.
2	Offices of Conrad & Conrad, LLP
3	Corpus Christi, Texas, December 1, YR-1, 10:00 A.M.

4

5

6

7   After having been sworn, Henry C. Baker testified:

8

9   Examination by Ms. Conrad:

10

11 Q: Would you state your name for the record?

12 A: Henry Carrington Baker, Jr.

13 Q: And your profession?

14 A: I'm the owner and president of Architronics, Inc. here in Corpus
15   Christi.

16 Q: Your age?

17 A: Forty-nine.

18 Q: Have you ever been deposed before?

19 A: No. This is my first time.

20 Q: Then you understand that the nature of this meeting is to take testimony
21   for the court proceedings initiated by my client, Mr. Edward Morgan,
22   against your company for age discrimination. I'll ask you questions,
23   then your own attorney, Mr. Hopkins, will ask you questions. I can ask
24   you more questions after that, as can he, in order. The questions and
25   answers will be recorded by the court reporter there, Ms. Brady. Do
26   you understand all that?

27 A: Yes.

28 Q: You came here today in response to a subpoena, is that so? Issued by
29   the district court?

30 A: Yes.

31 Q: And you understand that you have sworn to tell the truth here today?

32 A: Yes.

33 Q: Do you have any reservations about that oath?

34 A: No.

35 Q: Are you on any medication, stimulants, or drugs, or do you have any
36   health problems that would interfere with your testimony today?

37 A: No.

38 Q: No health problems?

39 A: Not that I know of.

40 Q: If you decide during questioning that you'd like to take a break, we'll do
41   that, all right?

42 A: Okay.

43 Q: If you don't understand a question, you have a right to, and should ask
44   for, clarification. Is that understood?

45 A: Yes.

46 Q: If you need me to repeat a question, you just ask, and if you want to
47   volunteer a clearer answer than you gave to a previous question, just
48   say so.

49 A: All right.

50 Q: At times, your attorney might object to a question you've been asked.
51   If so, he'll tell you whether to answer or not. The objection will be put
52   into the record by the court reporter and a judge will decide if your
53   answer can be used at trial. Do you understand that?
54 A: Yes.
55 Q: Was there anything unclear about what I just told you?
56 A: No. I understand.
57 Q: So you can think of no reason why you cannot give full and accurate
58   testimony here today?
59 A: No.
60 Q: All right, then, let's begin. You said you own and are president of
61   Architronics, Inc. here in Corpus Christi. What's the business of that
62   company?
63 A: We're architects. We provide design services for upscale design projects
64   in the metropolitan area, in Victoria, and in the surrounding counties
65   of southeast Texas. Of course, we've done projects all over the state and
66   in Louisiana too. We did an aquarium in New Orleans not long ago.
67 Q: How long have you been with Architronics?
68 A: My brother and I purchased the firm from its founder, Thompson
69   Williams, about seven years ago. He'd started it in YR-14, but the
70   business was limited to Corpus Christi then. We incorporated and
71   expanded it to a small branch office in Victoria about five years ago.
72 Q: Is your brother an active part of the company like yourself?
73 A: No, he's a co-owner, but he leaves the management to me. He lives in
74   Victoria.
75 Q: But you're an architect yourself?
76 A: Yes.
77 Q: Where did you train?
78 A: At UT Austin. I got a master's degree there as well.
79 Q: Do you only manage the company now, or do you design too?
80 A: Both. That is, I often decide overall design concepts; but a great deal of
81   what I do is management.
82 Q: And how many people do you employ? Architects, I mean.
83 A: Thirty total. Twenty-four here and six in the Victoria office.
84 Q: What kind of hierarchies does your employee structure have? I mean,
85   what are the differences in titles and responsibilities?
86 A: Well—other than the support staff—there are some staff architects, who
87   do computer design. Then above them are the project managers, who keep
88   things on time and within budget. They're on the same level with both the
89   senior designers, who decide the look of the project, and the job captains,
90   who ensure the functionality of the work—that is, that it actually does what
91   it's designed to do. Above all of them are the principal architects, like myself
92   and the senior vice presidents, who have the final word on overall design.
93 Q: And the Plaintiff was at what level?
94 A: He had a special role. He was a senior Design Specialist. He
95   drew wonderful construction detail and was great about making
96   sure that the designs were functional. He had some job captain
97   responsibilities as well. Elizabeth Allen had similar responsibi-
98   lities. They were somewhat familiar with an older CAD system,

99		called *VeriCad*, and used it. But they didn't implement it very much
100		in their presentations to clients. They relied on their drawings
101		primarily.
102	Q:	All right. We'll return to him in a moment. But tell me about the
103		company. What's been its history?
104	A:	Oh. I'd say we've done well. We've grown a lot and are quite large
105		for an architecture firm here in the state. When we bought the firm,
106		it was a traditional architecture firm. We did all the technical work
107		ourselves—prepared construction drawings and wrote the specs for
108		the projects. We would administrate contracts for clients—site visits
109		and all—and would administrate projects, as well as other services.
110		Basically, the whole range of things that architecture firms do. But
111		we've taken the business in a new direction over the years. We've
112		started more and more to provide only the design aspect, and entered
113		into agreements with other practices for the technical things. In other
114		words, we've become a kind of upscale "boutique" firm known for our
115		superior aesthetics and creativity. We've designed museums, high-end
116		restaurants and retail stores in metropolitan areas, civic showplaces,
117		headquarters for various institutes, expensive residences—that kind
118		of thing. It's a competitive business, but we've done well. All in all.
119	Q:	So you'd say you're successful.
120	A:	Well, we work hard. It's a hard business. We've had our rough spots,
121		like anybody else. Our biggest difficulties came last year.
122	Q:	Let's turn to that then. Are you speaking of the downturn that led to
123		Mr. Morgan's dismissal?
124	Mr. Hopkins:	Objection. That's at issue.
125	Q:	I'll rephrase that. The downturn that led to the event that's in contention
126		today.
127	A:	Yes, that was our biggest downturn.
128	Q:	When did you first perceive difficulties? That is, when did they first
129		come to your attention?
130	A:	About—I don't know exactly—but I'd say October of YR-2.
131	Q:	What was the nature of the change?
132	A:	Well, we realized that we weren't getting the numbers of contracts that
133		we had been. We were losing out on bids and referrals. This is a very
134		competitive business. You have to be able to design special spaces and
135		buildings in a variety of ways, depending upon the particular client.
136		You can't just make cookie-cutter plans. And you have to find out about
137		new projects and court them. You know. Get them to notice you. Like
138		any other business, we need to have some work in the pipeline, as it
139		were. Even if you have a big project, once it's done, if there isn't enough
140		in the planning stages, you're in trouble.
141	Q:	So you seek out clients?
142	A:	Some come by referrals, but we make presentations too.
143	Q:	How did this problem come to your attention in the fall of YR-2?
144	A:	My Chief Financial Officer—Philip Whitlow—brought this negative
145		trend to my attention in our quarterly meeting in October of YR-2. Not
146		that I hadn't noticed myself, of course. I mean, I knew we were falling
147		off in our contracts.
148	Q:	What justifies a determination that something's a negative trend,
149		then? When you have to deal with it in the way that you chose? Does
150		that make it a negative trend?
151	A:	You mean the restructuring?

40

152 Q: I mean the elimination of Mr. Morgan's job.

153 A: Well, that was in the spring of YR-1.

154 Q: When? When did you meet?

155 A: Let's see. My notes—let me look at my notes. We met on May 26. We meet
156   every month, but we met then about the urgency of the financial picture.

157 Q: Who was at that meeting?

158 A: Me, and Philip Whitlow, and Jane Fletcher, who's the head of the
159   Victoria office.

160 Q: What happened at that meeting?

161 A: Well, Philip said we were losing out again and again on jobs. He also
162   pointed out how tight our budget was. Then Jane said she thought
163   she knew why we were falling behind in client development. We'd
164   decided against buying a new state-of-the-art CAD system about a
165   year before.

166 Q: A what?

167 A: A CAD system. A computer-assisted design system. It had come out
168   the year before and was uniquely tailored to the kinds of special work
169   we do.

170 Q: What's it called? This CAD system.

171 A: *Quixotic 3000*. It came out in YR-3, around mid-year. It's a system that's
172   quite complex. It enables fast, incredibly precise, detailed renderings—
173   almost like holograms, they're so precise. It's quite expensive too, around
174     $20,000, what with the program and all the agreements and the new
175   equipment. We had thought that we could get by without it. But Jane
176   said that we were losing too much business to competitors who had it.
177   If you use it right—efficiently—it cuts costs for clients dramatically. I had
178   feared at the time that we'd made the wrong decision about it, but—you
179   know—I hadn't wanted to admit that. I'm sorry to say, but my decision
180   not to buy it in the first place may have caused all these difficulties, and
181   I hate that. But there was nothing to do at the time but look long and
182   hard at the alternatives, which there didn't seem to be any. And Jane
183   convinced me we just weren't competitive anymore.

184 Q: You didn't consider any other possibility for your problems? That was
185   the only solution, this CAD program? I mean, there were no other
186   allocations of resources that you looked to?

187 A: Well. I suppose that's a matter of opinion, whether we could have saved
188   money some other way. But it was determined in our business judgment
189   that this was the cause of our problems.

190 Q: So the only reason for your downturn was the design group that
191   Mr. Morgan was in charge of?

192 A: I'm not saying there weren't some other—efficiencies—we needed to
193   make. We're making them now. For example, we're no longer going to
194   an important conference in Germany—one on design aesthetics and
195   materials—that we used to attend, in order to economize. But the main
196   problem was not economizing. It was getting new business. I mean, you
197   can save money all you want, but at some point there's no more new
198   money coming in for you to save. It doesn't matter how thrifty you are
199   if there's nothing to be thrifty about.

200 Q: What other efficiencies then, did you make? What else did you
201   eliminate?

202 A: Well. I don't know right now. I can't say right at this minute.

203   Q: So since this was the only solution, you bought this program—
204   *Quixotic*—and decided to implement it?
205   A: We did. We had a big presentation coming up. It was for a multiple
206   building complex in Dallas—several art galleries and a music education
207   center—all surrounding a set of botanical gardens. We needed all
208   hands—everybody—able to help us out going forward. The license for
209   the program allowed for its use only in the Corpus Christi office. Time
210   was of the essence.
211   Q: When did you buy it?
212   A: In July. After the fourth. July 6, YR-1.
213   Q: You bought the program on July 6, YR-1, but did you tell anyone what
214   you were doing? Anyone that you let go? Specifically, Mr. Morgan?
215   A: No.
216   Q: Why not?
217   A: We didn't know then how to handle the situation. We were thinking it
218   through and didn't want to be premature about the ramifications.
219   Q: But after he left, when did you actually implement the program?
220   A: It turns out that we just got it going at the start of last October, YR-1.
221   In early October. We had some trouble with our hardware and we had
222   some other implementation difficulties.
223   Q: So a program you bought in July, that was key to what you call a need for
224   immediate turnaround, was not actually operational until October?
225   A: Yes. But we didn't plan that, of course. It just happened that way.
226   Q: But neither the Plaintiff nor Ms. Allen was told or trained in the time
227   prior to the "restructuring," as you call it? They weren't given a chance
228   to train on this program?
229   A: We didn't see that as an option. Not at that time last summer. We
230   didn't see training, I mean, as an option. We were of the opinion that
231   we had to get things going immediately. The big bid was coming up and
232   we needed to be competitive immediately on it. So we decided we had to
233   bring in someone that was already trained.
234   Q: So when did you make that decision—that you needed a new person?
235   A: Before the holiday. Before July 4, YR-1. I looked at the figures that
236   Philip gave me. He had his recommendations, of course, and I listened
237   to him. But it was up to me. I poured over the options and decided this
238   is what we had to do to survive—get the program—get a person who
239   knew how to run it and could train our people in it.
240   Q: But you didn't tell anyone about it?
241   A: No. Like I said, we were feeling our way through how to handle it.
242   Q: And what did those duties entail, the ones related to this new job?
243   A: Well, the main thing, the crucial thing, was the program. Knowing
244   how to run it, implement it, and train others in its use. We hope that
245   Margaret—Ms. Ellison—will be able to bring all of our designers up
246   to speed on it eventually. She'll do in-house training, when things
247   even out.
248   Q: But doesn't she still do what Mr. Morgan did? Doesn't she still meet
249   with clients and explain designs?
250   A: Yes, she does that too.
251

252   Q: Don't her duties overlap with the duties Mr. Morgan had?

253   A: To a degree.

254   Q: Isn't "building design" overlap? And the meetings with clients? Isn't all
255   that the same thing that Mr. Morgan did for you—for ten years?

256   A: Yes.

257   Q: So there is overlap. It's not a completely different job, is it?

258   A: Well—naturally—it's a design job. There's going to be some overlap in
259   design jobs, since they're by nature "design" jobs. But I'd say they were
260   totally different in that this new position involved skills that the old
261   jobs didn't. Crucial skills.

262   Q: How much is overlap?

263   Mr. Hopkins: Objection—calls for speculation.

264   Q: It's not speculation. He knows these two jobs—the old and the new—he
265   can surely estimate whether she does the same thing Mr. Morgan
266   did—the percentage of overlap.

267   Mr. Hopkins: He can answer rough percentages.

268   A: Well, I guess—and it's just a guess—she does 50% of the old job and
269   50% of the new tasks, related to the program. But that will change
270   in the future, as the job becomes more and more related to the
271   programming.

272   Q: Just to clarify though, she is doing 50% of the work that is still client-
273   related, as well as the modeling job that Mr. Morgan did. Correct?

274   A: Approximately. That's just a guess.

275   Q: And didn't Mr. Morgan get "outstanding" marks from you on his
276   evaluations as far as customer relations go?

277   A: Yes. He's very good at that.

278   Q: And what were the evaluations of the people in that group, the design
279   group that Mr. Morgan was a part of.

280   A: All good for the two architects. But there were troubles with
281   Mr. McKenna, their administrative assistant and draftsman. Mr. Morgan
282   knew about those problems and alerted us to them.

283   Q: Weren't Mr. Morgan's reviews excellent, as a matter of fact? And he was
284   noted for his customer relations expertise in a special commendation
285   by you in YR-2, isn't that so?

286   A: Yes. As I said, he's great at that. And he deserved that. I don't deny
287   that.

288   Q: Why did the evaluations change, Mr. Baker?

289   A: What's that?

290   Q: The employee evaluations. They changed in May to include questions
291   about computer training and familiarity with the latest design
292   models.

293   A: Because the job was changing. We thought that was important to add.

294   Q: But you hadn't trained anyone, so how could they be evaluated on it?

295   A: Well, training is available. You can get it in continuing education
296   courses. We pay for that.

297   Q: Did you tell people, including the two people impacted, that you wanted
298   them to be trained in the latest design programs?

299   A: I'm not sure. We encourage a lot of things.

300   Q: When did you decide to eliminate the positions?

301   A: It was part of that July decision. I decided there wasn't enough time
302   to train anyone, and that the old duties were just not part of the new
303   business we needed to be. A reduction in force was in order.

304   Q: Who made the decision?

305   A: Me. Nobody else. I'm the president. It comes down to me.

306   Q: But no other positions were eliminated in your reduction in force?

307   A: It wasn't necessary. It was a painful thing as it was. I didn't *want*
308   to let Ed—Mr. Morgan—go. On August 2, YR-2, I offered both him
309   and Elizabeth other positions. She of course decided to retire instead.
310   But I wanted Mr. Morgan to take the job in Victoria. It came down
311   to numbers. Down to our survival. It became a matter of eliminating
312   three jobs and replacing them with one so as to save all the other jobs—
313   including my own. They were the only two—Ed and Elizabeth—who
314   didn't know much about CAD stuff—who didn't like it much and who
315   stuck to their way of working. And we had just moved past that kind
316   of old way. Everybody else was sophisticated in CAD usage. It wasn't
317   the same business as it was when they started. The kind of technical
318   work that Ed's group did—and did beautifully—was not what we did
319   so much anymore. We valued what they could do, but the business
320   had changed. They would've been starting from too far back. And as
321   I said, they weren't without options. They were both offered other
322   roles—ones that were very much like the jobs that they had then.

323   Q: Have you ever let anyone else go?

324   A: No. Not one of my architects, no. My office manager has let some assistants
325   go, for underperforming or breaching protocols, but no architects.

326   Q: Only this group? The two in Corpus Christi.

327   A: Yes.

328   Q: But of the three members in that group, one, Mr. Morgan, was
329   fifty-seven, and the other, Ms. Allen, was sixty-one.

330   A: I know that. And Mr. McKenna was thirty-five. Did you know that?

331   Q: But the two architects were the oldest people in your employ, isn't that true?

332   A: Yes. It happened to be.

333   Q: Has Mr. Morgan ever gone for computer training?

334   A: I'm not sure. I think he's kept up in his field. I've always said that.

335   Q: But he has never refused training, has he?

336   A: Not that I'm aware of. He stuck to the old *VeriCad* system though.
337   He always said he preferred it.

338   Q: Have you ever insisted on it or offered it, training I mean?

339   A: No, but I pay for the continuing education of my architects.

340   Q: Why did you deal with these three employees in three different ways?

341   A: I—I just considered that it was appropriate. They were three people
342   with three different circumstances. They were individuals and I treated
343   them as such.

344   Q: But the reduction in force happened to affect only the oldest members
345   of your employ, true?

346   A: No. Mr. McKenna was not one of the oldest.

347   Q: Weren't you planning to let Mr. McKenna go, anyway? Before August?

348   A: That was a possibility. His performance wasn't what we'd hoped.

349   Q: Did you consider laying Mr. Morgan off too?

350	A:	No. I wanted him to take the job in Victoria.
351	Q:	But that job was a demotion, wasn't it?
352	A:	Well, it's all we had. An Assistant Design Specialist. But it was at
353		largely the same salary and exactly the same benefits.
354	Q:	In Victoria, which is at least an hour and a half drive away?
355	A:	Yes.
356	Q:	And there was no expense account with this job. True?
357	A:	Yes.
358	Q:	And a lesser title?
359	A:	Yes, but it's all we had. I told you. We were in trouble financially.
360	Q:	Why did you give Mr. Morgan only three days to consider your offer?
361	A:	Things were moving fast. I thought he needed to make a break with
362		us if that was what he thought best. There wasn't room or time for
363		negotiations on it.
364	Q:	You were aware that this is Mr. Morgan's hometown though, and that
365		he has a daughter here?
366	A:	Yes.
367	Q:	You're aware that she was recently widowed and has a small son that
368		Mr. Morgan and his wife help care for?
369	A:	I knew that. It was all tough. None of it was pleasant, I assure you. I sent him
370		an email after I broke the news, telling him that I'd thought this through
371		and that it was best. We have a history of transferring people to the other
372		office and vice versa, if need be. We've done it before—two years ago—when
373		two of our folks went up to Victoria because we needed them there.
374	Q:	And they lived here in Corpus Christi, these two people?
375	A:	Well, no actually. I think both of them lived about halfway between here
376		and Victoria. Maybe a little closer to Victoria, come to think of it.
377	Q:	And did they work primarily in the Corpus Christi office?
378	A:	No. They worked in both offices, though they were hired to work in the
379		Corpus Christi office primarily. But they wound up working up in Victoria
380		a good deal of the time. They were eventually transferred to that office
381		permanently—but the point is that we have a history of transfers.
382	Q:	You also knew that Mr. Morgan's benefits were not yet fully vested,
383		didn't you? And that there were nine months left before they would be?
384	A:	That's why I offered him the job in Victoria. Our program vests by
385		length of service. I didn't want that to happen to him. I didn't have to
386		offer him that job.
387	Q:	How did you know of Ms. Ellison?
388	A:	I didn't. We put an ad in the national trades and she applied, in mid-July.
389		She lived in Houston and responded. She called us and was the first
390		person we talked to about it.
391	Q:	When was that?
392	A:	Late August. Let me look—August 15, YR-1.
393	Q:	She's eight years younger than Mr. Morgan, isn't that so?
394	A.	I have no idea how old she is. I didn't ask.
395	Q:	What was her training?
396	A:	She had similar training to Ed—Mr. Morgan. But she
397		was up to speed in *Quixotic*. She was a trainer for the
398		program, in fact, and she would save us money in future

45

399		training costs. We could do it all in-house, and wouldn't have to bring
400		in somebody from *Quixotic* to train our people. That's what really sold
401		the deal. She hit the ground running.
402	Q:	She came with benefits though? That is, she has no benefits through
403		your company?
404	A:	She has her benefits outside the company, yes. But that had nothing to
405		do with her hire.
406	Q:	Has there been a change in business because of the *Quixotic* program?
407		Did you get the bid you had anticipated with this program?
408	A:	Well, as I said, we weren't fortunate in getting it up and running.
409	Q:	You mean you didn't even use the program on this bid that required the
410		elimination of these jobs?
411	A:	As it turns out, no. But as I said, we didn't know we'd run into
412		difficulties. We told the companies that we had it and would be able
413		to implement it soon, though. It was instrumental in our getting part
414		of that business. We didn't get all of it, but enough. We got one of the
415		three buildings to be built.
416	Q:	But let me understand, none of the *Quixotic* skills were used in getting
417		this business?
418	A:	No.
419	Q:	And that bid for the one building was secured when?
420	A:	In November.
421	Q:	What date?
422	A:	I'm not sure. I can check.
423	Q:	But four months after the elimination of these jobs?
424	A:	Yes.
425	Q:	Mr. Baker, do you remember hearing the comments said to Mr. Morgan
426		and Ms. Allen, about their ages?
427	A:	I'm not sure what you mean.
428	Q:	I mean, you were aware that Mr. Morgan and Ms. Allen were called the
429		"Leonardo" group by younger members of the staff?
430	A:	Oh, I knew that.
431	Q:	And you knew that your CFO, Mr. Whitlow, had called them that?
432	A:	Yes.
433	Q:	What did you understand that comment to mean?
434	A:	Well. It's slang. You know—as in "Leonardo da Vinci." It's just a name
435		for draftsmen who do things in a—I don't know—in an older, traditional
436		way, I suppose. "Protractor and compass" style. It's just a joke.
437	Q:	You mean in an outdated way?
438	A:	Some would say.
439	Q:	Did you ever call them that?
440	A:	No.
441	Q:	Did you stop others from doing so?
442	A:	No. It was just a joke. Ed never complained about it. Neither did
443		Elizabeth. And they were never said in any way related to this
444		restructuring of our firm. Anyhow, Philip called *me* the same thing, as
445		a matter of fact, from time to time. I didn't care.
446		
447		

448 Q: You knew your Vice President, Stephen Abernathy, had a heated
449   exchange with Mr. Morgan last January, in which Mr. Abernathy
450   stated that Mr. Morgan was part of the "old way" of thinking and had
451   been around since protractors were invented?

452 A: I knew that. But they both lost their cool that day. Edward condescended
453   to Stephen, from what I was told—patronized his knowledge of what's
454   best for the company. But they put it behind them.

455 Q: To clarify, this is the same Stephen Abernathy who gave an interview
456   last summer with the local newspaper touting a new youthful
457   orientation to your business model, isn't that so?

458 A: He was just trying to say interesting things to the reporter—to highlight
459   our commitment to CAD. He was excited about the program and what it
460   could do for our business. Everybody in the firm was sure this would solve
461   our problems—everybody but Edward's group. They're the only ones who
462   resisted this initiative. So I'm not going to criticize the way Stephen put
463   things. He meant no harm, and it had nothing to do with my decision.

464 Q: But you had disagreements about some policies with Mr. Morgan, isn't
465   that true?

466 A: Yes, but they weren't major.

467 Q: What were their natures?

468 A: Oh, he didn't want to implement a new pricing structure for expense
469   accounts. He didn't think that was good for business. He thought that
470   taking clients out to dinner and drinks was still the best way to secure
471   business.

472 Q: In a May YR-1 meeting, didn't you tell him that he was being stubborn,
473   and that he would have to change? That "all the young people in the
474   firm" understood this?

475 A: I might have. Like I said, he didn't like the direction we were taking
476   with the firm. He didn't like the "boutique" idea at all, and he often
477   said the emphasis on aesthetics was taking us away from being a "real"
478   architecture firm. He was undercutting Stephen Abernathy's attempts
479   to change our image, too—something I didn't appreciate. But it had
480   nothing to do with my decision.

481 Q: When you sprang the news of his job elimination, didn't you tell him
482   that times had changed and everybody had to accept such things—that
483   your "time" was coming too?

484 A: I might've put it that way. I was trying to put things as gracefully as I could.

485 Q: You knew about your obligations under the ADEA, didn't you?

486 A: Yes.

487 Q: Did you consult anyone about them?

488 A: With my attorney. In May. I wanted to follow the law in the event we
489   had to make some changes. I wanted to follow the law.

490 Q: Thank you. No further questions.

491
492 Examination by Mr. Hopkins:

493 Q: What impact did you foresee *Quixotic 3000* having on your business
494   model?

495 A: It would change it totally, as far as design goes. It *is* changing it. Right
496   now. We've become competitive again.

497 Q: On what do you base that?

498 A: On my business judgment. I had to make the decision for my company.
499   You always risk being wrong, but that's the risk of business.

500 Q: How popular was the decision?

501 A: Oh, very. I was the last one to get on the bandwagon, I'm ashamed to
502   say. The other architects had been petitioning me to buy a program like
503   this for quite some time. All but Edward's group, that is.

504 Q: What motivated your decision to eliminate the design group in the
505   headquarters?

506 A: The new model. The new model that would, and I believe will yet, save
507   us. It was an efficiency-based decision to reduce a redundant work
508   force. It was a decision made at a time of great import for my company.
509   That was all that motivated my choices. And as it's my business—my
510   investment—my sweat and blood—a decision about what's best for it
511   should be left up to me. Period.

512 Q: Thank you. No further questions.

513

514 (End of Deposition: 11:20 a.m., December 1, YR-1.)

515

516 ### Certificate of Stenographer

517

518 I, Sarah M. Brady, certified stenographic reporter for the court,
519 CSR No. 4674, do hereby certify that I reported in Stenograph notes the
520 foregoing proceedings, and that they have been edited by me, or under
521 my direction and the foregoing transcript contains a full, true, complete
522 and accurate transcript of the proceedings held in this matter, to
523 the best of my knowledge. I further certify that this transcript of the
524 proceedings truly and correctly reflects the exhibits, if any, offered by
525 the respective parties.

526   In witness, I have subscribed my name on this 1st day of December,
527 YR-1.

528

529   *Sarah M. Brady*
530   Sarah M. Brady

1	Deposition of Mary Margaret Ellison
2	Offices of Conrad & Conrad, LLP
3	Corpus Christi, Texas, October 18, YR-1, 10:00 A.M.
4	
5	
6	After having been sworn, Mary M. Ellison testified:
7	
8	Examination by Ms. Conrad:
9	
10	Q: Please state your name and age for the record
11	A: Mary Margaret Ellison. I'm forty-nine.
12	Q: Have you been deposed before, Ms. Ellison?
13	A: Yes, about five years ago with relation to an accident I was witness to.
14	Q: It was a lawsuit?
15	A: Yes. But it settled before the trial.
16	Q: How many times were you deposed with regard to that lawsuit?
17	A: Just once.
18	Q: But you're familiar with the process?
19	A: Yes.
20	Q: As you may recall, this testimony is sworn, and is subject to use in the
21	lawsuit of Edward Morgan against his former employer, Architronics,
22	Inc., which is your current employer.
23	A: I understand that.
24	Q: And you have sworn to tell the truth? No qualms about that oath?
25	A: No qualms.
26	Q: I'll ask questions of you, and your attorney may object to those
27	questions and will tell you whether to answer or not. But those
28	questions will nevertheless be part of the record for a judge to
29	decide upon. Everything is being taken down by the court reporter
30	over there. You understand?
31	A: Yes.
32	Q: Mr. Hopkins may ask you some questions later, and then I can ask you
33	more if necessary. All right?
34	Q: You're under no medication or suffering from any illness that would
35	prevent your unqualified testimony today, is that right?
36	A: No.
37	Q: If you need a break we'll take one. And if you need clarification on
38	anything, just ask me. Okay?
39	A: Okay.
40	Q: Now, Ms. Ellison, you are currently employed by Architronics, Inc.
41	in Corpus Christi, isn't that so?
42	A: Yes.
43	Q: In what capacity?
44	A: As the CAD Specialist—that's Computer-Assisted Design Specialist.
45	Q: Is that a common title of your business?
46	A: I was given it when I started.
47	Q: You were a CAD Specialist before you started with the company?
48	
49	

50	A:	Well, yes, but under a different title. They just called me a Design Specialist
51		at my old job in Houston. It was a small firm of four architects.
52	Q:	So people aren't really called "CAD Specialists" then.
53	A:	I haven't heard it before. They—my bosses—made it up for me when
54		I came on.
55	Q:	You mean you started with that title or it was given to you recently?
56	A:	Given to me recently.
57	Q:	How recently?
58	A:	I don't recall exactly. Maybe a few months ago.
59	Q:	And when were you contacted by Architronics?
60	A:	About two weeks after I responded to an ad in the regional trade magazine.
61		It asked for someone with advanced CAD training, which I have.
62	Q:	In your estimation, how long does a person need to learn Quixotic
63		proficiently?
64	A:	Well, that depends on the person. The company itself would give the
65		best range of time regarding that. I used to refer such questions to
66		the information supplied on their website.
67	Q:	What else did the ad ask for? I mean the one that you answered in the
68		paper?
69	A:	It wanted someone dynamic and able to work with a vibrant, up-and-
70		coming business.
71	Q:	Who contacted you?
72	A:	Mr. Baker did.
73	Q:	And you met with him when?
74	A:	August 15, YR-1.
75	Q:	Who else did you meet with?
76	A:	Just him and the CFO, Mr. Whitlow.
77	Q:	What was the substance of the meeting?
78	A:	They said they'd looked at my resume and seen my *Quixotic* abilities.
79		They needed someone immediately to come help them in Corpus Christi.
80		They said they weren't going to beat around the bush—that they were
81		losing business, but they felt that this ability—the CAD work I could
82		offer clients—would make them competitive again. They said I could get
83		onto the ground floor of something big and growing if I came to help.
84	Q:	Did the ad say anything about training people?
85	A:	No.
86	Q:	But you've been training people since you came?
87	A:	Yes, some of that—just brushing people up on it. Honestly, I hadn't expected
88		that to be part of my job, but they seemed to want that when we met.
89	Q:	Were you told anything about the people that you replaced?
90	A:	No. I wasn't told anything about them.
91	Q:	How long did it take you to learn the program?
92	A:	I went to school for it for a month—at my own expense—and it was
93		about another month before I got the hang of it. Maybe another two
94		months before I became really proficient. I then decided to get extensive
95		training and become a certified instructor for the company. I did that
96		for a few months just before I took this job.
97	Q:	Why did you quit?
98	A:	It was just too much travel.

99   Q: And what do you mean you "went to school" for it?

100 A: Well, I took an intensive study course in it at a design college

101   in Houston—at The Massey School of Design. I was thinking at

102   the time I heard about it that it would revolutionize the design

103   work I was interested in, which is the very high-concept work that

104   Architronics does.

105 Q: How would it revolutionize that?

106 A: Well, it's complicated. But it enables the designer to give all kind of

107   views and offer multiple formatting, depending on the client's stated

108   desires. If they want a change—the client that is—this program can

109   project it in no time, and with very little expense. Much less than the

110   old models, and certainly faster than the drafting we did before—the

111   kind of thing that the company was doing until they got this program.

112 Q: There were problems though, at Architronics, in the implementation of

113   the program?

114 A: Yes, there were. It took an unexpected amount of time to get it going.

115   I was surprised that they had connectivity problems. It was all

116   frustrating for everybody. But we were able to assure the clients that it

117   would be ready in time to give them the savings that were included in

118   the bids. We guaranteed that.

119 Q: Now, Ms. Ellison, do you do work with the program exclusively?

120 A: No. I do traditional work too.

121 Q: How much would you say is traditional in nature?

122 A: Oh, I don't know. I guess, since I've started up, I've done a lot of

123   traditional work—maybe even more of that than the CAD work. But

124   that's because we weren't yet operational with the program.

125 Q: Yes, how many presentations have you been a part of or made yourself?

126 A: Well, not that many. I've never done any by myself. I'd worried about

127   that when I applied for the job, but it wasn't a concern apparently.

128 Q: What is your professional training, Ms. Ellison?

129 A: I have a B.A. in architecture from Louisiana State University.

130   I graduated in YR-28.

131 Q: Any graduate degrees?

132 A: No.

133 Q: And how long have you been an architect and where have you practiced?

134 A: I practiced in Houston for about eight years. When my children were

135   small, I stopped and raised them. Then I came back in YR-13 to a practice

136   there in town—a small three-person firm. I did mostly drafting work.

137   I was there for several years until I got interested in computer-assisted

138   design. I became a local representative for a company—not Quixotic,

139   Inc.—for a few years and also taught at a local community college. That

140   was before I went with Quixotic. And then, of course, I took this job.

141 Q: How many presentations to clients have you made over the years?

142 A: How many have I made myself?

143 Q: Yes. How much work with clients have you done?

144 A: Well, not that much. I was never a senior designer or a job manager.

145 Q: Have you made any presentations with clients since starting with

146   Architronics?

147 A: No, not by myself.

148 Q: Do you have your benefits through your current employer?
149 A: No, I have them though my husband's company.
150 Q: Thank you. No further questions.
151
152 (End of Deposition: 11:20 a.m., October 18, YR-1.)
153
154
155 **Certificate of Stenographer**
156
157 I, Sarah M. Brady, certified stenographic reporter for the court,
158 CSR No. 4674, do hereby certify that I reported in Stenograph notes the
159 foregoing proceedings, and that they have been edited by me, or under
160 my direction and the foregoing transcript contains a full, true, complete
161 and accurate transcript of the proceedings held in this matter, to
162 the best of my knowledge. I further certify that this transcript of the
163 proceedings truly and correctly reflects the exhibits, if any, offered by
164 the respective parties.
165   In witness, I have subscribed my name on this 18th day of October,
166 YR-1.
167
168   *Sarah M. Brady*
169   Sarah M. Brady
170

1   Deposition of Edward J. Morgan
2   Offices of Hopkins, Eliot, and Jones
3   Corpus Christi, Texas, September 15, YR-1, 10:00 A.M.
4
5
6   After having been sworn, Edward J. Morgan testified:
7
8   Examination by Mr. Hopkins:
9
10   Q: For the record, state your name and age.
11   A: Edward James Morgan, 57.
12   Q: Have you ever been deposed before, Mr. Morgan?
13   A: No, I haven't.
14   Q: All right. For clarity's sake, a deposition, which you're about to give,
15   is sworn testimony that can be used in the court proceeding you've
16   instituted for age discrimination against Architronics, Inc. I'll ask you
17   questions, then your own attorney may do the same, and so forth. The
18   court reporter, Ms. Berringer, will record all this. Do you understand?
19   A: Yes.
20   Q: You came here today in response to a subpoena from the federal district
21   court here in Corpus Christi, correct?
22   A: Yes.
23   Q: And you've sworn to tell the truth today?
24   A: Yes.
25   Q: Do you have any qualifications about that oath?
26   A: No.
27   Q: Are you on any medication, stimulants, or drugs, or do you have any
28   health problems that would interfere with your testimony?
29   A: No.
30   Q: We can take a break any time you'd like. You just say so. All right?
31   A: Yes.
32   Q: If you don't understand a question, I'll rephrase it for you. Or if you
33   didn't hear it, I'll be glad to repeat it. Just ask.
34   A: Okay.
35   Q: Now, your attorney has the right to object to something I ask, and she'll
36   tell you whether to proceed with a response. The objection, at any rate,
37   will go into the record for the court to decide whether the substance of
38   the statement is admissible at trial. Okay?
39   A: Yes.
40   Q: Was there anything unclear about what I just told you?
41   A: No. I understand.
42   Q: So you can think of no reason why you cannot give full and accurate
43   testimony here today?
44   A: No.
45   Q: All right then. Mr. Morgan, are you currently employed?
46
47
48
49

50   A. No. I was employed for ten years at Architronics here in town, but as
51   you know, I was let go last August.
52   Q: What was your position there, before you left?
53   A: I was a Design Specialist.
54   Q: And what was your training for that position?
55   A: I received a B.A. degree from Texas Tech in YR-37. I worked for a
56   local firm for five or six years before I moved to Dallas and started
57   a partnership with a school friend for ten years. Then I moved back
58   home, as my wife wanted to come back to be close to her family.
59   I'd worked with the founder of this company as a colleague for years—
60   not Mr. Baker—his predecessor, Mr. Williams—and he asked me to join
61   his group, Architronics, in YR-11.
62   Q: And the duties involved with that position?
63   A: Well, they were varied. I'm a real architect, if I may say so. I know how
64   to do detailed hand-drawn construction renderings, detailed specs, etc.
65   I also oversaw functionality of projects—I did that for both my projects
66   and Elizabeth's. I met with prospective clients and came up with
67   proposals. I was involved in the conceptual side of things.
68   Q: Were you ever involved or asked to take any additional training while
69   with the company?
70   A: I was. Of course, I had to keep up with my continuing education hours.
71   We're required to do that to keep our licenses valid in the state. And
72   I kept abreast of all the new developments in technology and all the
73   latest advancements in material designs.
74   Q: Did you ever take any courses in computer-assisted design—in CAD
75   programs?
76   A: I took one. I know how to do it, by and large. I use—as did Ms. Allen—
77   *VeriCad*, which I admit is a more elementary design program. It's not
78   the latest thing, but it's sufficient. The point is, that if I could do that,
79   I could do anything that I had to do. No computer skills are too complex
80   for me.
81   Q: But there are more advanced programs that you have not learned,
82   whereas others in the firm do in fact know them, isn't that so?
83   A: Yes. As I said, there are other things to being an architect. I got the
84   job done with my models. I made great presentations and hardly ever
85   lost a contract. I also had to concern myself with crucial things—like
86   the functionality of the buildings. These days, a lot of people who
87   are computer jockeys don't know how a building works. It can't just
88   look good on paper. It has to work. So while they were training on
89   all these things, I was making sure the buildings we designed would
90   actually stand up on their own.
91   Q: Isn't it true, though, that everyone at the firm consistently used more
92   advanced CAD programs than your group, and utilized them on a
93   routine basis?
94   A: They employed that technology more than we did, yes. They liked the
95   advanced gadgetry.
96   Q: And didn't all of the Corpus Christi office architects send a memo last
97   winter, directed to Mr. Baker, advocating the purchase of *Quixotic*?
98   Signed by all but your group?
99   A: I didn't sign it, and neither did Elizabeth. We had a different view as to the
100   indispensability of such things, which I should hope we're entitled to have.

101	Q:	Tell me, who paid for the continuing education you took?
102	A:	The company did.
103	Q:	Did you take any extra training, on your own? Any CAD training?
104	A:	No, I didn't have that much time. I was involved with more important
105		things.
106	Q:	Have you ever been trained in *Quixotic 3000*?
107	A:	No.
108	Q:	Had you heard of it before August of last year?
109	A:	No.
110	Q:	Were you aware that three of Architronics' major competitors own and
111		utilize that program?
112	A:	No.
113	Q:	Were you aware that training, according to designers' statements in
114		the sales literature on *Quixotic 3000*, can take up to a month, and
115		proficiency is achieved only after several months?
116	A:	As I said, I wasn't aware of the program. I have been asked to learn
117		things—programs in modeling—that are complex, and I've never
118		refused or failed to achieve a mastery of them. My job reviews as to
119		adaptability were always good.
120	Q:	But your job reviews never anticipated CAD, did they?
121	A:	No. But I'm confident I could've mastered it.
122	Q:	In an even shorter time than the designers of the program say?
123	A:	Well, I don't claim that. But in at least that much time.
124	Q:	But didn't Mr. Baker state to you in your meeting of August 2, YR-1
125		that the business was in severe financial decline, and that there was
126		simply no time to learn the program?
127	A:	Yes. He said that. I don't know if it was true or not.
128	Q:	You knew the business was on hard times though?
129	A:	I knew there had been talks of cut-backs. But I thought that was
130		just belt-tightening stuff. Lowering expense accounts and cost-saving
131		measures. No new hires. I didn't know they were going to lay us all off.
132		In fact, at the time, the rumor was that they were just going to limit
133		our raises, and this was the excuse we were being given. I don't think
134		the company was—or is—in any real difficulties.
135	Q:	Well, Mr. Morgan, you weren't laid off, were you?
136	A:	I think I was.
137	Q:	You were offered a job—basically a transfer—to Victoria, at nearly the
138		same salary. Isn't that so?
139	A:	In my view, it was not the same job.
140	Q:	But the difference in salary—a matter of $3000 a year—was because
141		that was the only job available right then, wasn't that so? And your
142		benefits would've stayed the same. Isn't that true?
143	A:	Yes, but I'd have to go through the disgrace of becoming an Assistant
144		Design Specialist, in a satellite office, after working as a Design
145		Specialist for ten years—and with reduced privileges—my expense
146		account would be curtailed—all of my old friends would know. Plus it
147		was over seventy-five miles away—more like ninety, all in all—from my
148		home. That's hardly a daily commute.
149	Q:	But weren't you told that this was the best the company could do, for
150		now?
151	A:	Yes.

55

152	Q:	And didn't you tell Mr. Baker that you'd "think it over"? You didn't
153		object or refuse it outright?
154	A:	I didn't know what to think. He—Mr. Baker—gave me three days to
155		think about it. And I was in shock. I hardly remember what I said that
156		day. I know that when I left the office, driving home, I realized all at
157		once that such a thing was impossible. And that it wasn't a real offer.
158		He—Mr. Baker—knew I couldn't leave town. My daughter's husband died
159		last year and she has a small child. My wife and I help support them.
160		We couldn't move and I couldn't drive over an hour and a half—with
161		that traffic between these two large cities—every day to work. On top of
162		that, I live twenty miles south of here, in Kingsville—my hometown.
163	Q:	So you had decided to refuse the offer immediately, as soon as you
164		drove off from work—you didn't take the whole three days to decide, as
165		you were asked?
166	A:	There was no point. I knew it was impossible, given my circumstances.
167	Q:	Have you ever opposed any of the company's business decisions?
168	A:	Well, it depends on what you mean by "opposed."
169	Q:	I'll clarify. Has the company ever asked you to do something and you
170		refused to do it?
171	A:	Well, we butted heads some, Mr. Baker and I did. Last May, he wanted
172		to cut back on the expense accounts. He was of the opinion that that
173		kind of client contact was uncalled for. And I wasn't fond of the way the
174		business was outsourcing the technical side of things. It was becoming
175		all design. I feared we were becoming all flash and no substance. But
176		that was just my opinion. I never refused to do anything I was asked,
177		and only wanted the best for the place.
178	Q:	Didn't you tell him that you were "too old to change"?
179	A:	I may have said that. I just meant that I didn't think it was—prudent—to
180		squander the good will of the company like that. Referrals are important,
181		and the happier the customers are with their experience, the more
182		they'll refer business your way when they're asked for opinions. But
183		he said that all the young people in the office were going along with it
184		and I was out of step. I also thought it unwise to outsource what was so
185		basic to the very idea of architecture—the technical aspect of things.
186	Q:	But you concede that it was within the company's rights to make such a
187		change, to move it in the direction they wanted? That's a business decision.
188	A:	I went along with it.
189	Q:	But what I'm asking is, you concede that the company has a right to
190		make decisions that it deems best for itself?
191	A:	I know business decisions have to be made, and sometimes hard
192		ones. But they have to be made fairly. They have to be made for the
193		right reasons.
194	Q:	How many people worked with you?
195	A:	Elizabeth Allen and Harris McKenna, the administrative assistant.
196	Q:	How long did they work there?
197	A:	Elizabeth had been there for about as long as I had. McKenna came
198		only a few years ago. He was our administrative assistant, though he
199		was an architecture student for a while and did some drafting work for
200		us as well.
201	Q:	Were you his supervisor?
202	A:	Yes, in a way. I couldn't hire or fire, but I oversaw his work.

203   Q: Were you involved in or privy to his yearly evaluations?

204   Q: I was. I also know that Ms. Allen always did exemplary work and
205   her evaluations were always strong. I didn't review her, as we were
206   colleagues, but I was privy to that knowledge, since she told me so.

207   Q: And Mr. McKenna?

208   A: There were problems with Mr. McKenna's performance.

209   Q: What kind of problems?

210   A: Well...Am I allowed to say that?

211   Ms. Conrad: Yes. You can say what you have knowledge of.

212   A: His work wasn't all we'd hoped. He wasn't as careful and didn't
213   produce the kind of detail we commanded. And he was often out sick.
214   Disproportionately so, it was felt.

215   Q: So when you learned that Mr. McKenna had been discharged, you were
216   not in disagreement with the company's decision?

217   A: Well—I don't suppose.

218   Q: You were part of that business decision yourself, if you were his
219   evaluator, weren't you?

220   A: I guess so. Yes. I agreed with it.

221   Q: No more questions.

222

223   Examination by Ms. Conrad:

224

225   Q: And how were your evaluations prior to August 2, YR-1?

226   A: Always excellent. I was commended in particular for my client
227   satisfaction.

228   Q: How did you learn of the news that you would be discharged?

229   A: I was surprised by it. I'd been out at a meeting all day and had returned
230   to the office. I was ambushed as I was leaving the office.

231   Q: Have there ever been any comments made to you about your age?
232   If so, by whom and—if you can recall—where and when were they
233   made?

234   A: Yes. The whole bunch of them referred to me and Elizabeth as the
235   "Leonardo" group—as though we were antiquated and old-fashioned.
236   They did that all the time—on too many occasions to relate. But one
237   day, last spring, Philip Whitlow called us that once on his way through
238   the office, while he was following Mr. Baker down the hall, and they
239   both smiled.

240   Q: Any other such instances?

241   A: Yes. Before that, I'd had a conflict with Stephen Abernathy, one of
242   the Vice Presidents—the one that was crazy for the CAD stuff and
243   even gave an interview to the newspaper last July about how "young"
244   they wanted to be around the place. He's a big friend of Whitlow's.
245   They have lunch together all the time. Anyhow, a year ago—last
246   January—Abernathy had heard how I was against the CAD push that
247   was taking hold of the place. He came into my office to confront me
248   about it. I told him what I thought and he called my view the "old way
249   of doing things" and decisions would be made by people who weren't
250   around when protractors were invented.

251   Q: What did you do then?

252 A: I told him I knew my rights. That I couldn't be talked to like that. I was
253   mad, I admit, and went around the office talking about seeing a lawyer.
254   I left some pamphlets around the place on age discrimination. But it
255   all seemed to blow over. Until August, that is.
256 Q: Anything else?
257 A: Yes. My last evaluation included questions about my computer design
258   capabilities. And on August 2, YR-1, Mr. Baker told me that "everyone's
259   'time' comes eventually," and that this was mine.
260 Q: What did you understand him to mean?
261 A: That it was time to retire me. That I was over the hill.
262 Q: Was anyone else present on August 2, YR-1 when you met with
263   Mr. Baker?
264 A: No.
265 Q: What did you say to Mr. Baker when he told you the news?
266 A: I asked him who else was being affected, and he said just my group.
267   And that shocked me, if things were as dire as he said. And I asked
268   him what was happening to Elizabeth, and he said she'd been offered
269   early retirement and had taken it. Well, I knew she had been thinking
270   of that anyway, and when I heard about McKenna, I wasn't surprised,
271   like I said. But the more I thought about it, the more it seemed like
272   McKenna was going to be let go anyway, and that he was an incidental
273   part of shuffling me and Elizabeth out the door.
274 Q: What do you mean by "shuffling you out the door"?
275 A: I mean getting us out—me with no real options and put in a position to
276   have to refuse their offer, and her on early retirement.
277 Q: Were you vested in your benefits plan, Mr. Morgan?
278 A: That's another thing. I was about nine months shy of fully vesting.
279 Q: And finally, you said earlier you didn't think the company was in
280   financial straits. Can you elaborate?
281 A: I mean that they paid bonuses and took trips and things. I don't think
282   that's consistent with a company in the trouble that they describe. It's
283   one thing to waste your own money—you're entitled to do that. But
284   you can't use your bottom line as a cooked up excuse for getting rid of
285   somebody you don't want around anymore.
286
287 Ms. Conrad: No more questions.
288
289
290 (End of Deposition: 11:20 a.m., September 15, YR-1.)
291
292
293
294
295
296
297
298
299
300

Certificate of Stenographer

301
302
303 I, Laura K. Berringer, certified stenographic reporter for the court,
304 CSR No. 6543, do hereby certify that I reported in Stenograph notes
305 the foregoing proceedings, and that they have been edited by me, or
306 under my direction and the foregoing transcript contains a full, true,
307 complete and accurate transcript of the proceedings held in this matter,
308 to the best of my knowledge. I further certify that this transcript of the
309 proceedings truly and correctly reflects the exhibits, if any, offered by
310 the respective parties.
311   In witness, I have subscribed my name on this 15th day of September,
312 YR-1.
313
314   *Laura K. Berringer*
315   Laura K. Berringer

In The
UNITED STATES DISTRICT COURT
FOR THE SOUTHERN DISTRICT OF TEXAS
Corpus Christi Division

Edward J. Morgan,
5678 Church Street   )
Kingsville, Texas 78363,   )
       Plaintiff,   )   Civil Action No. 12345
       v.   )   Complaint and Jury Demand
Architronics, Inc.,   )
9876 Upper Broadway Street)
Corpus Christi, Texas 78401,)
      Defendant.   )

DEFENDANT'S MOTION FOR SUMMARY JUDGMENT

Defendant, Architronics, Inc., by its undersigned counsel, moves this Court, pursuant to Rule 56(b) of the Federal Rules of Civil Procedure, for an Order granting summary judgment in its favor on Plaintiff's Complaint. Support for this motion is set forth in the accompanying Memorandum of Law, the affidavit attached thereto, and the attached depositions of Edward J. Morgan, Henry C. Baker, and Mary Margaret Ellison.

Respectfully submitted,

G. Mark Hopkins
Hopkins, Eliot, and Jones
Attorneys at Law
567 Harrison Place South
Corpus Christi, Texas 78470
Telephone: 316-555-4312
email: hejlawfirm.com
Attorneys for Defendant,
Architronics, Inc.

Dated: February 22, YEAR

Certificate of Service

I HEREBY CERTIFY that I caused a copy of the foregoing Motion for Summary Judgment to be sent via U.S.P.S. Express Mail, postage prepaid, and to be delivered by hand this 22nd day of February, YEAR, to counsel for the Plaintiff, Rebecca A. Conrad, Conrad & Conrad, LLP, Suite 1056, Commerce Place, Corpus Christi, Texas 78470.

G. Mark Hopkins
Bar No. 0066778
Hopkins, Eliot, and Jones
Attorneys at Law
567 Harrison Place South
Corpus Christi, Texas 78470
316-555-4312
email: hejlawfirm.com
Attorneys for Defendant,
Architronics, Inc.

EXHIBIT A

In The
UNITED STATES DISTRICT COURT
FOR THE SOUTHERN DISTRICT OF TEXAS
CORPUS CHRISTI DIVISION

Edward J. Morgan,
5678 Church Street   )
Kingsville, Texas 78363,   )
      Plaintiff,   )   Civil Action No. 12345
      v.   )
Architronics, Inc.,   )
9876 Upper Broadway Street   )
Corpus Christi, Texas 78401,)
      Defendant.   )

AFFIDAVIT

The undersigned affiant, being first duly sworn, hereby says:

1. I hereby state that I am over the age of eighteen, suffer no legal disabilities, have personal knowledge of the facts set forth below, and am competent to testify.
2. I hereby state that I have been employed as Chief Financial Officer ("CFO") of Defendant, Architronics, Inc., a Texas corporation (the "Company") since January, 1, YR-9.
3. I hereby state that the Company operates on a calendar-year basis. The Company is a closely-held corporation.
4. I hereby state that as CFO of the Company, I have custody of the financial records of the Company, draft and oversee quarterly budgets, am responsible for overall financial administration of the Company, including planning, organizing, directing and leading all business matters, and report to, and make recommendations to, the President of the Company quarterly basis and on an as-needed basis.
5. I hereby state that during the period beginning October 1, YR-2 and ending October 1,YR-1, the company made the following unbudgeted expenditures:

    a. YR-2 year-end performance bonuses to President Henry C. Baker; Senior Vice President Jane Fletcher; and Vice President Stephen Abernathy.

    b. Travel expenses of President Henry C. Baker, Senior Vice President Jane Fletcher, and Vice President Stephen Abernathy; to design conference in Munich, Germany, December, YR-2.

    c. November, YR-2 construction costs associated with new façade for Corpus Christi headquarters building.

This, the 1st day of December, YR-1.

Philip W. Whitlow

Philip W. Whitlow, CFO
Architronics, Inc.

Sworn to and subscribed before me this
The 1st of December, YR-1.

Allison M. McManus
Allison M. McManus, Notary Public
My commission expires: December 19, YR+2

In The
UNITED STATES DISTRICT COURT
FOR THE SOUTHERN DISTRICT OF TEXAS
Corpus Christi Division

Edward J. Morgan,	)	
5678 Church Street	)	
Kingsville, Texas 78363,	)	
Plaintiff,	)	Civil Action No. 12345
v.	)	
Architronics, Inc.,	)	
9876 Upper Broadway Street	)	
Corpus Christi, Texas 78401,	)	
Defendant.	)	

PLAINTIFF'S RESPONSE TO DEFENDANT'S MOTION FOR SUMMARY JUDGMENT

Plaintiff Edward J. Morgan, by his undersigned counsel, hereby responds to Defendant's Motion for Summary Judgment, and requests that this Honorable Court deny Defendant's Motion with Prejudice, and in support thereof provides the attached Memorandum of Law in Opposition to Defendant's Motion for Summary Judgment, the attached Exhibit A, and the attached depositions of Edward J. Morgan, Henry C. Baker, and Mary Margaret Ellison.

Respectfully submitted,

Rebecca A. Conrad
Conrad & Conrad, LLP
Suite 1056, Commerce Place
Corpus Christi, Texas 78470
Telephone: 316-555-2134
email: conrad@conrad.com
Attorneys for Plaintiff, Edward J. Morgan

Dated: March 1, YEAR

Certificate of Service

I HEREBY CERTIFY that I caused a copy of the foregoing Plaintiff's Response to Defendant's Motion for Summary Judgment and Memorandum of Law in Opposition to Defendant's Motion for Summary Judgment to be sent via U.S.P.S. Express Mail, postage prepaid, and to be delivered by hand this 1st day of March, YEAR, to counsel for Defendant, G. Mark Hopkins, Hopkins, Eliot, and Jones, 567 Harrison Place South, Corpus Christi, Texas, 78470.

Respectfully submitted,

Rebecca A. Conrad
Conrad & Conrad, LLP
Suite 1056, Commerce Place
Corpus Christi, Texas 78470
Telephone: 316-555-2134
email: conrad@conrad.com
Attorneys for Plaintiff, Edward J. Morgan

EXHIBIT A

Highlights of *Quixotic 3000*

(from *Quixotic 3000* website: www.Quixotic3000.com/highlights)

Quixotic 3000 is the most advanced rendering application available in the world today. It provides the architectural designer the capacity to design in 3D, edit and navigate projects within the 3D format, as well as animate and make presentations from within the rendering itself. The images are as close to "hologram" quality as any commercial application has ever been able to accomplish.

All building materials and the latest design concepts can be utilized in the virtual project, and projections based on even the latest trial technology are available with the program.

Details are scale-sensitive and the environment in which the project is situated can be simulated with astounding quality.

All information regarding the building is stored in a central database and any changes made in a particular view/aspect are automatically updated in all others.

Information can be shared with colleagues, and multiple designers can work on different aspects of the project at different times or simultaneously. The program will co-operate with existing information-sharing programs.

Design elements such as apertures and load-bearing supports are specific to the environment in which they exist.

Document integrity is ensured and all editing and restructuring of virtual projects is automatically updated.

Training: Quixotic, Inc. understands that attendant with the dynamic possibilities that the program affords the modern firm are a general set of concerns. Namely, how difficult is the program to learn and implement? While courses in the program are widely available at most design schools, Quixotic, Inc. has a staff of skilled professionals—architects who have obtained training certification through our own standard-setting protocols—that will provide on-site training and continuous support. Skill levels with any program may vary, and therefore impact the time necessary to master the application. Nonetheless, it is estimated that under the approximately month-long tutelage of our professionals, the average architect, with a standard familiarity in computer-assisted design programming, will be proficient by two months succeeding training.

Assignment 7

ORAL DEFENSE OF ADEA MOTION'S BRIEF

Conrad & Conrad, LLP
Suite 1056, Commerce Place
Corpus Christi, Texas 78470
Telephone: 316-555-2134
Facsimile: 316-555-1211
conrad@conrad.com

INTEROFFICE MEMORANDUM

From: Rebecca A. Conrad
To: Associate Attorney
Re: Edward Morgan Matter
Date: Today, YEAR.

Prepare an oral argument of the motion's brief written with regard to the above-referenced matter. The argument will be held in the federal court of the Southern District of Texas. The judge will allot the time limits and the argument protocols set out in the attachment to this letter.

Rac/bb

Hopkins, Eliot, and Jones
Attorneys at Law
567 Harrison Place South
Corpus Christi, Texas 78470
Telephone: 316-555-4312
Facsimile: 316-555-2111
hejlawfirm.com

INTEROFFICE MEMORANDUM

From: G. Mark Hopkins
To: Associate Attorney
Re: Architronics Matter
Date: Today, YEAR.

Prepare an oral argument of the motion's brief written with regard to the above-referenced matter. The argument will be held in the federal court of the Southern District of Texas. The judge will allot the time limits and the argument protocols set out in the attachment to this letter.

GMH: mc

Assignment 8

APPELLATE BRIEF: ADEA

Conrad & Conrad, LLP
Suite 1056, Commerce Place
Corpus Christi, Texas 78470
Telephone: 316-555-2134
Facsimile: 316-555-1211
conrad@conrad.com

INTEROFFICE MEMORANDUM

From: Rebecca A. Conrad
To: Associate Attorney
Re: Edward Morgan Matter
Date: Today, YEAR.

As you know, Judge Winston has handed down her order with regard to the above-referenced matter. An appeal has been requested and granted. The order and all appellate documents are attached.
Review these materials and draft an appellate brief to the Fifth Circuit.

Rac/bb

Hopkins, Eliot, and Jones
Attorneys at Law
567 Harrison Place South
Corpus Christi, Texas 78470
Telephone: 316-555-4312
Facsimile: 316-555-2111
hejlawfirm.com

INTEROFFICE MEMORANDUM

From: G. Mark Hopkins
To: Associate Attorney
Re: Architronics Matter
Date: Today, YEAR.

As you know, Judge Winston has handed down her order with regard to the above-referenced matter. An appeal has been requested and granted. The order and all appellate documents are attached.
Review these materials and draft an appellate brief to the Fifth Circuit.

GMH: mc

PLEADINGS: MOTION TO DISQUALIFY

Conrad & Conrad, LLP
Suite 1056, Commerce Place
Corpus Christi, Texas 78470
Telephone: 316-555-2134
Facsimile: 316-555-1211
conrad@conrad.com

INTEROFFICE MEMORANDUM

From: Rebecca A. Conrad
To: Associate
Date: Today, YEAR.
Re: Edward J. Morgan

Edward J. Morgan is a fifty-seven-year-old resident of Kingsville, Texas, a town near Corpus Christi. He lives at 5678 Church Street, Kingsville, Texas 78363 and is a former employee of Architronics, Inc., a Texas corporation with offices in Corpus Christi and Victoria, Texas. Architronics address is 9876 Upper Broadway Street, Corpus Christi, Texas 78401.

Architronics, Inc. specializes in high concept architectural design. It employs thirty architects in its two branches. Its main branch is in Corpus Christi, and the other is in nearby Victoria.

For ten years, Morgan had held the position of Design Specialist, the job description of which included technical drafting for building designs and meeting with clients.

On August 2, YR-1, Morgan returned from a day-long meeting with a client and was called into the office of company president, Henry Baker. Baker informed Morgan that the company had to make some immediate changes. He said that, as Morgan knew, Architronics had been in financial straits of late. The last quarter showed that the situation had grown dire. Architronics' ability to compete in its local markets was being eclipsed by its lack of computer-assisted design (CAD) capabilities. Specifically, a particular computer program—*Quixotic 3000*—key to servicing clients' design needs cost-effectively, was possessed by Architronics' competitors and had been determined as directly responsible for the company's loss of business. The program would have to be bought and implemented immediately—within the next month or two—if the company were to survive. Morgan was informed that though this was a decision no one wanted to make, Architronics had decided it was necessary to hire someone already proficient in *Quixotic*. As a result, a reduction in force was in order, and the positions held by Morgan and his immediate group of co-workers, Elizabeth Allen, 61, and Harris McKenna, 35, would be eliminated. The new position would replace those held by Morgan, Allen, and McKenna.

Earlier in the day, Allen had been offered early retirement, which she had decided to take. McKenna had been let go. Morgan was offered the opportunity to work in Victoria at the same basic salary and benefits, though as an Assistant Design Specialist with a reduced expense account. Victoria is approximately seventy-five miles from Corpus Christi. Morgan lives in Kingsville, Texas, which is twenty minutes south of Corpus Christi. Because of the exigency of the circumstances, the job offer in Victoria had to be accepted in three days.

Morgan decided against the offer. The daily commute would be too long, and he and his wife did not want to move from their hometown because they assist their daughter, who is raising her child alone subsequent to the death of her husband. He also considered the job a demotion. He was surprised by the news, as to his knowledge there had been no indication that a reduction in force was going to be implemented. There were rumors of hard times, but nothing as drastic as this. He has since learned that the replacement worker, Margaret Ellison, is a forty-nine-year-old woman, proficient in *Quixotic 3000*, and certified to train others in its use. Morgan had never refused any training that he was asked to undergo, though he had resisted some changes as he did not think they were good business decisions by his superiors. His job evaluations prior to the news had been good, though the last set of evaluations had changed to include questions about his proficiency in computer skills.

As part of his ADEA claim, Morgan first will have to show that he was discharged. I already have an associate looking into a retaliatory discharge claim, so I would like for you to determine whether Morgan can satisfy the "discharge" element under a theory of constructive discharge. If so, draft a complaint for his ADEA claim. Your Complaint should allege jurisdictional facts and facts supporting all elements of the prima facie case, and it should conclude with a prayer for relief/demand for judgment.

Hopkins, Eliot, and Jones
Attorneys at Law
567 Harrison Place South
Corpus Christi, Texas 78470
Telephone: 316-555-4312
Facsimile: 316-555-2111
hejlawfirm.com

INTEROFFICE MEMORANDUM

From: G. Mark Hopkins
To: Associate
Re: Architronics, Inc.
Date: Today, YEAR.

Edward J. Morgan is a fifty-seven-year-old resident of Kingsville, Texas, a town near Corpus Christi. He lives at 5678 Church Street, Kingsville, Texas 78363 and is a former employee of Architronics, Inc., a Texas corporation with offices in Corpus Christi and Victoria, Texas. Architronics address is 9876 Upper Broadway Street, Corpus Christi, Texas 78401.

Architronics, Inc. specializes in high concept architectural design. It employs thirty architects in its two branches. Its main branch is in Corpus Christi, and the other is in nearby Victoria.

For ten years, Morgan had held the position of Design Specialist, the job description of which included technical drafting for building designs and meeting with clients.

On August 2, YR-1, Morgan returned from a day-long meeting with a client and was called into the office of company president, Henry Baker. Baker informed Morgan that the company had to make some immediate changes. He said that, as Morgan knew, Architronics had been in financial straits of late. The last quarter showed that the situation had grown dire. Architronics' ability to compete in its local markets was being eclipsed by its lack of computer-assisted design (CAD) capabilities. Specifically, a particular computer program—*Quixotic 3000*—key to servicing clients' design needs cost-effectively, was possessed by Architronics' competitors and had been determined as directly responsible for the company's loss of business. The program would have to be bought and implemented immediately—within the next month or two—if the company were to survive. Morgan was informed that though this was a decision no one wanted to make, Architronics had decided it was necessary to hire someone already proficient in *Quixotic*. As a result, a reduction in force was in order, and the positions held by Morgan and his immediate group of co-workers, Elizabeth Allen, 61, and Harris McKenna, 35, would be eliminated. The new position would replace those held by Morgan, Allen, and McKenna.

Earlier in the day, Allen had been offered early retirement, which she had decided to take. McKenna had been let go. Morgan was offered the opportunity to work in Victoria at the same basic salary and benefits, though as an Assistant Design Specialist with a reduced expense account. Victoria is approximately seventy-five miles from Corpus Christi. Morgan lives in Kingsville, Texas, which is twenty minutes south of Corpus Christi. Because of the exigency of the circumstances, the job offer in Victoria had to be accepted in three days.

Morgan decided against the offer. The daily commute would be too long, and he and his wife did not want to move from their hometown because they assist their daughter, who is raising her child alone subsequent to the death of her husband. He also considered the job a demotion. He was surprised by the news, as to his knowledge there had been no indication that a reduction in force was going to be implemented. There were rumors of hard times, but nothing as drastic as this. He has since learned that the replacement worker, Margaret Ellison, is a forty-nine-year-old woman, proficient in *Quixotic 3000*, and certified to train others in its use. Morgan had never refused any training that he was asked to undergo, though he had resisted some changes as he did not think they were good business decisions by his superiors. His job evaluations prior to the news had been good, though the last set of evaluations had changed to include questions about his proficiency in computer skills.

As part of his ADEA claim, Morgan first will have to show that he was discharged. I already have an associate looking into a retaliatory discharge claim, so I would like for you to determine Morgan's case for making a claim of constructive discharge. Afterwards, draft an answer to his complaint, which is attached.

BRIEF: MOTION TO DISQUALIFY

Hopkins, Eliot, and Jones
Attorneys at Law
567 Harrison Place South
Corpus Christi, Texas 78470
Telephone: 316-555-4312
Facsimile: 316-555-2111
hejlawfirm.com

INTEROFFICE MEMORANDUM

From: G. Mark Hopkins
To: Associate
Date: Today, YEAR.
Re: Edward J. Morgan, ADEA Claim v. Architronics, Inc.

As you are aware, Edward J. Morgan in the above-styled case has filed a Motion to Disqualify me from representation of Architronics, Inc. in the above-referenced matter.
Please draft a memorandum of law in opposition to that Motion to Disqualify Counsel.

Conrad & Conrad, LLP
Suite 1056, Commerce Place
Corpus Christi, Texas 78470
Telephone: 316-555-2134
Facsimile: 316-555-1211
conrad@conrad.com

INTEROFFICE MEMORANDUM

From: Rebecca A. Conrad
To: Associate
Date: Today, YEAR.
Re: Edward J. Morgan ADEA Claim v. Architronics, Inc.

As you are aware, we have filed a Motion to Disqualify G. Mark Hopkins from representing the defendant, Architronics, Inc., in the above-styled case.
Please draft a memorandum of law in support of that Motion to Disqualify Counsel.

In The
UNITED STATES DISTRICT COURT
FOR THE SOUTHERN DISTRICT OF TEXAS
Corpus Christi Division

Edward J. Morgan	)	
5678 Church Street	)	
Kingsville, Texas 78363,	)	
Plaintiff,	)	Civ. Action No. 12345
v.	)	
Architronics, Inc.	)	
9876 Upper Broadway Street	)	
Corpus Christi, Texas 78401,	)	
Defendant.	)	

PLAINTIFF'S MOTION TO DISQUALIFY COUNSEL

Pursuant to the Federal Rules of Civil Procedure, movant, Edward J. Morgan, plaintiff in the above cause of action, files this motion to disqualify attorney G. Mark Hopkins, who represents Architronics, Inc., the defendant in this action. In support of this motion, movant shows the court the following:

1. Plaintiff, Edward J. Morgan resides at 5678 Church Street, City of Kingsville, County of Kleberg, State of Texas, 78363.
2. Defendant, Architronics, Inc., is a corporation organized and existing under the laws of the State of Texas with its principal place of business located at 9876 Upper Broadway Street, City of Corpus Christi, County of Nueces, State of Texas.
3. G. Mark Hopkins, a managing partner with Hopkins, Eliot, and Jones, Attorneys at Law, 567 Harrison Place South, Corpus Christi, Texas 78470, has been lead counsel representing defendant in this action.
4. From August 25, YR-1 until the present, Ellen H. Ambrose has been employed as a paralegal by Hopkins, Eliot, and Jones.
5. From September 25, YR-2 until July 30, YR-1, Ellen H. Ambrose was an employee of Robinson and Porter Attorneys in Victoria Texas, working as a paralegal. During that time, Ellen H. Ambrose conducted a real estate transaction in which plaintiff was the buyer of certain property near Victoria, Texas. In the course of this transaction, Ellen H. Ambrose received confidential information as to the plaintiff's intentions for the use of the purchased property.
6. There is a substantial relationship between the subject of the real estate transaction Ms. Ambrose closed at Robinson and Porter Attorneys and the instant case.

7. At no time has plaintiff executed a waiver of his rights to object to subsequent employment of Ellen Ambrose by clients with adverse interests to Plaintiff.

8. As knowledge gained by Ellen H. Ambrose, as an employee of Hopkins, Eliot, and Jones, is imputed to G. Mark Hopkins, managing partner of Hopkins, Eliot, and Jones, the representation of defendant by G. Mark Hopkins against plaintiff is a violation of the duty of fidelity that is imposed on G. Mark Hopkins as a member of the Texas Bar pursuant to the Texas Disciplinary Rules of Professional Conduct, by the Canons of Professional Ethics of the American Bar Association, and by the Code of Professional Responsibility of the American Bar Association.

9. The parties have conferred, but counsel cannot agree as to the disposition of the motion.

10. G. Mark Hopkins should therefore be disqualified from maintaining or participating in this action on behalf of defendant.

Wherefore, movant respectfully requests the following relief:

1. An order temporarily enjoining G. Mark Hopkins and Hopkins, Eliot, and Jones from representing defendant in this case until this matter can be determined by the court;

2. An order permanently disqualifying G. Mark Hopkins and Hopkins, Eliot, and Jones from representing defendant in this case; and

3. Any further relief that the court determines is just and proper.

In support of this motion, Plaintiff provides the attached Memorandum of Law.

Respectfully submitted,

Rebecca A. Conrad
Rebecca A. Conrad
Attorney-in-Charge
Texas Bar No. 0075759
S.D. Texas Bar No. 20020220
Conrad & Conrad, LLP
Suite 1056, Commerce Place
Corpus Christi, Texas 78470
Telephone: 316-555-2134
Facsimile: 316-555-1211
Email: conrad@conrad.com
Attorney for Plaintiff, Edward J. Morgan

Dated: December 30, YR-1

Certificate of Service

I HEREBY CERTIFY that I caused a copy of the foregoing Plaintiff's Motion to Disqualify Counsel to be sent via U.S.P.S. Express Mail, postage prepaid, and to be delivered by hand this 30th day of December, YR-1, to counsel for Defendant, G. Mark Hopkins, Hopkins, Eliot, and Jones, 567 Harrison Place South, Corpus Christi, Texas, 78470.

Respectfully submitted,

Rebecca A. Conrad
Rebecca A. Conrad
Attorney-in-Charge
Texas Bar No. 0075759
S.D. Texas Bar No. 20020220
Conrad & Conrad, LLP
Suite 1056, Commerce Place
Corpus Christi, Texas 78470
Telephone: 316-555-2134
Facsimile: 316-555-1211
Email: conrad@conrad.com
Attorney for Plaintiff, Edward J. Morgan

In The
UNITED STATES DISTRICT COURT
FOR THE SOUTHERN DISTRICT OF TEXAS
Corpus Christi Division

Edward J. Morgan	)	
5678 Church Street	)	
Kingsville, Texas 78363,	)	
Plaintiff,	)	Civ. Action No. 12345
v.	)	
Architronics, Inc.	)	
9876 Upper Broadway Street	)	
Corpus Christi, Texas 78401,	)	
Defendant.	)	

DEFENDANT'S RESPONSE TO PLAINTIFF'S MOTION TO DISQUALIFY COUNSEL

Defendant, Architronics, Inc., by its undersigned counsel, hereby responds to Plaintiff's Motion to Disqualify Counsel, and requests that this Honorable Court deny Plaintiff's Motion with Prejudice, and in support thereof provides the attached Memorandum of Law in Opposition to Plaintiff's Motion to Disqualify Counsel.

Respectfully submitted,

G. Mark Hopkins
G. Mark Hopkins
Attorney-in-Charge
Texas Bar No. 0066778
S.D. Texas Bar No. 943866
Hopkins, Eliot, and Jones
Attorneys at Law
567 Harrison Place South
Corpus Christi, Texas 78470
Telephone: 316-555-4312
Facsimile: 316-555-2111
email: hejlawfirm.com
Attorneys for Defendant,
Architronics, Inc.

Dated: January 2, YEAR

Certificate of Service

I HEREBY CERTIFY that I caused a copy of the foregoing Defendant's Response to Plaintiff's Motion to Disqualify Counsel to be sent via U.S.P.S. Express Mail, postage prepaid, and to be delivered by hand this 2nd day of January, YEAR, to counsel for the Plaintiff, Rebecca A. Conrad, Conrad & Conrad, LLP, Suite 1056, Commerce Place, Corpus Christi, Texas 78470.

G. Mark Hopkins
G. Mark Hopkins
Attorney-in-Charge
Texas Bar No. 0066778
S.D. Texas Bar No. 943866
Hopkins, Eliot, and Jones
Attorneys at Law
567 Harrison Place South
Corpus Christi, Texas 78470
Telephone: 316-555-4312
Facsimile: 316-555-1211
email: hejlawfirm.com
Attorneys for Defendant,
Architronics, Inc.

1   UNITED STATES DISTRICT COURT SOUTHERN DISTRICT
2   OF TEXAS CORPUS CHRISTI DIVISION
3
4
5
6   Edward James Morgan,   )
7   PLAINTIFF,   )
8   )   Civ. Action
9   v.   )   No. 12345
10 Architronics, Inc.,   )
11   DEFENDANT.   )
12
13
14
15   Transcript of Proceedings before the Honorable M. Leigh Barksdale
16
17   The matter of the above-styled case was heard before the Honorable
18 M. Leigh Barksdale on January 5, YEAR at 10:00 a.m.
19
20 Appearances:
21
22   Rebecca A. Conrad, Esq.
23   For the Plaintiff
24
25   Edward J. Morgan,
26   Plaintiff
27
28   G. Mark Hopkins, Esq.
29   For the Defendant
30
31   Ellen H. Ambrose
32   Witness
33
34 COURT REPORTER:
35
36   McKenzie Smith, CSR, RDR, CRR
37   3230 Rarity Avenue
38   Corpus Christi, Texas
39   Phone: (316) 555-7698
40
41
42
43
44
45
46
47
48
49

50   PROCEEDINGS
51   January 5, YEAR
52

53 THE COURT: All right. Let's have everybody present identify themselves.
54 We'll start with the left side of the room here—those here for the Plaintiff.
55

56 MS. CONRAD: Rebecca Conrad, your Honor. Here as Plaintiff's counsel.
57

58 MR. MORGAN: Edward Morgan.
59

60 THE COURT: And you're the plaintiff, Mr. Morgan?
61

62 MR. MORGAN: Yes, your Honor.
63

64 THE COURT: Okay, that's it for the Plaintiff's side. No one else?
65

66 MS. CONRAD: No your Honor.
67

68 THE COURT: Then on the other side. Who do we have for the Defendant?
69

70 MR. HOPKINS: Mark Hopkins your Honor, counsel for the Defendant
71 Architronics, Inc.
72

73 THE COURT: And finally—are you—ma'am—are you with Architronics
74 or—
75

76 MS. AMBROSE: No, your Honor. I'm Ellen Ambrose. I'm an employee of
77 Mr. Hopkins' law firm.
78

79 THE COURT: All right. I see. Yes. Now that's what we're here about today.
80 These proceedings, for the record, are attendant to a motion to disqualify
81 Defendant's counsel, Mr. Hopkins, made by the Plaintiff. I called this
82 hearing in order to obtain, in the easiest, most efficient manner, all of the
83 facts necessary for my decision on that matter. As this motion is being made
84 relative to an active lawsuit for age discrimination brought by the Plaintiff
85 against his former employer, the Defendant, and because this entire matter
86 has come to a head over the last few weeks—at least to my understanding,
87 that's the case—we're having this hearing to get all of the evidence out
88 right now. It's a serious thing, a motion to disqualify counsel, and it needs
89 to be decided expeditiously and correctly. That's so the case can either
90 proceed with present counsel, or Defendant can obtain new counsel in the
91 event I decide that the motion should be granted. To that end, I've asked
92 for everyone that has knowledge about this matter—for both sides—to be
93 present here today, and you've both assured me that's the case. Correct?
94

95 MR. HOPKINS: Yes, your Honor.
96

97 MS. CONRAD: Yes, your Honor.
98

99 THE COURT: Now, for the record, Mr. Morgan is a former employee of
100 the architecture firm, Defendant Architronics, Inc. Mr. Morgan has filed a
101 federal age discrimination suit with this court under the Age Discrimination
102 in Employment Act. This motion to disqualify Mr. Hopkins is being made
103 relating to matters arising from his firm's employment of Ms. Ambrose.
104 Have I set that out correctly, Ms. Conrad?
105
106 MS. CONRAD: That's right, your Honor.
107
108 THE COURT: And that motion was made on December 30, YR-1, for the
109 record. Mr. Hopkins, you have that motion?
110
111 MR. HOPKINS: I do, your Honor.
112
113 THE COURT: All right, and let the record reflect that I've talked with
114 counsel for both parties in my chambers to go over procedural matters.
115 I understand that subsequent to this hearing, both parties will be
116 presenting briefs for my consideration prior to my decision. Unless either
117 of you want to make an opening statement, I think we can move right to
118 the examinations.
119
120 MR. HOPKINS: No statement.
121
122 MS. CONRAD: None, your Honor.
123
124 THE COURT: One last thing. Mr. Morgan is not required to disclose anything
125 particular that is detrimental to his age discrimination suit in order to
126 prove that the Defendant's counsel should be disqualified, but he must
127 make a case for that disqualification nevertheless. Is that understood?
128
129 MR. HOPKINS: Yes.
130
131 MS. CONRAD: Yes.
132
133 THE COURT: Then Ms. Conrad, call your first witness.
134
135 MS. CONRAD: The Plaintiff calls Edward James Morgan.
136
137 [Mr. Morgan is sworn]
138
139   DIRECT EXAMINATION OF EDWARD JAMES MORGAN
140
141 MS. CONRAD: Mr. Morgan, would you state your name, age, address, and
142 profession for the court.
143
144 MR. MORGAN: Edward James Morgan, fifty-seven years old. I'm a resident
145 of Kingsville, Texas. I live there with my wife.
146

147 MS. CONRAD: And how far from Corpus Christi is Kingsville?
148
149 MR. MORGAN: Oh, twenty miles south, I guess.
150
151 MS. CONRAD: Your profession?
152
153 MR. MORGAN: I'm an architect. Have been an architect my whole life.
154 I received a B.A. degree from Texas Tech in YR-37. I worked for a local firm
155 for five or six years, then I moved to Dallas and started a partnership with
156 a school friend for ten years. I moved back here, as my wife wanted to come
157 back to be close to her family. I'd worked with the founder of this company
158 as a colleague for years—not Mr. Baker, who's the current president—but
159 his predecessor—and he asked me to join his group, Architronics. So I was
160 with them for around ten years, up until this recent thing.
161
162 MS. CONRAD: Your position with Architronics?
163
164 MR. MORGAN: I was a Design Specialist. I drafted construction renderings,
165 detailed specs, etc. I also oversaw the functionality of projects—I did that
166 for both my projects and for the projects of my colleague, Elizabeth Allen.
167 I met with prospective clients and came up with proposals. I was involved
168 in the conceptual side of our company's high-end designs.
169
170 MS. CONRAD: How many architects are there at the firm?
171
172 MR. MORGAN: Thirty total. Twenty-four here in Corpus Christi, and six
173 in the Victoria, Texas office.
174
175 MS. CONRAD: What's been your relationship with your employer?
176
177 MR. MORGAN: For about a year or so, strained. They were implementing
178 this new computer-assisted design initiative there—and they'd made a
179 big capital outlay to purchase an expensive program called *Quixotic 3000*.
180 And in addition, they'd begun to make a push for a "high-tech image" in
181 everything they did. We—Elizabeth and I—stated our objections. We just
182 thought the persona was getting bigger than the job—that the image of the
183 place had taken over the business of the place, if you will. And being the
184 oldest two people in the firm, we were the targets of—
185
186 MR. HOPKINS: Objection, your Honor. They're trying to wage the age
187 discrimination suit right here and now.
188
189 THE COURT: Ms. Conrad, you'll need to limit your questions, and Mr. Morgan,
190 your answers, to things directly related to the motion to disqualify. Mr.
191 Morgan doesn't need to get into proving his age discrimination suit today.
192
193 MS. CONRAD: All right, your Honor. But we must of course touch upon things
194 that show a relationship between our motion and the substantive lawsuit.
195

196 THE COURT: Yes, but the relationship between the matters can be shown
197 without Mr. Morgan making allegations of age discrimination.
198
199 MS. CONRAD: All right, your Honor. Now, Mr. Morgan, tell the court about
200 how your association with Architronics ended.
201
202 MR. MORGAN: Well, on August 2 of last year—August 2, YR-1, that is,
203 Henry Baker, the president of the firm, wanted to see me just as I was
204 coming back to the office from a business call. He let me know that because
205 of the financial straits the firm was in lately, they'd decided to reduce the
206 force in our office here. He said there were some Assistant Design Specialist
207 positions in the Victoria office, though, which he was offering me and
208 Elizabeth. Now, Elizabeth just went ahead and took early retirement—she
209 didn't even consider what they were offering. But I didn't want to do that—
210 they put me in this position and I didn't deserve it.
211
212 MR. HOPKINS: Objection. This is getting into the age discrimination
213 merits again.
214
215 MS. CONRAD: Your Honor, on this point, that's precisely why it's relevant.
216 It directly relates to Mr. Morgan's prima facie case in his age discrimination
217 suit—that he was constructively discharged from Architronics' employ. We
218 contend that Mr. Morgan's argument in that regard is directly impacted by
219 information known to Ms. Ambrose, Mr. Hopkins' employee, and therefore
220 is grounds for Mr. Hopkins' disqualification. There's no way for your Honor
221 to get the information you need to make this decision unless Mr. Morgan
222 testifies about the context of his release from his employer.
223
224 THE COURT: Objection overruled. Proceed.
225
226 MS. CONRAD: All right, Mr. Morgan. You were saying they wanted you to
227 go to the Victoria office. Victoria, Texas is—what? —about an hour and a
228 half north of Corpus Christi?
229
230 MR. MORGAN: Yes. And the job was as an Assistant Design Specialist,
231 not a Design Specialist. It did carry just about the same salary and all
232 the same benefits, but the title would be different and I'd lose my expense
233 account. And that commute would of course be far too much to undertake
234 every day—considering that I already live south of here.
235
236 MS. CONRAD: Did you think of relocating?
237
238 MR. MORGAN: I can't. I have a daughter whose husband died last year. She
239 lives in Kingsville and my wife and I help take care of her son. Besides, it's
240 my hometown. Why should I have to relocate? At any rate, I was shocked.
241
242 MS. CONRAD: Now, tell the court how you know Ellen Ambrose.
243
244 MR. MORGAN: I met her about six months ago. Ms. Ambrose closed my
245 loan for me.
246

247 MS. CONRAD: What kind of loan?
248

249 MR. MORGAN: A house purchase. I bought a place up on Lake Texana, in
250 the Lake View development, and she closed the loan for me. At the time, she
251 was with Robinson and Porter, a real estate closing firm in Victoria. She
252 closed loans for the bank that financed my purchase, Texas National.
253 The Robinson firm has also represented me in other real estate transactions
254 in the past, in which I was the seller.
255

256 MS. CONRAD: How far is Lake Texana from Victoria?
257

258 MR. MORGAN: About twenty-five miles north. I guess. Around that.
259

260 MS. CONRAD: And how involved was she in the transaction itself?
261

262 MR. MORGAN: Very. She was the one that set up the sale and the closing
263 and did all the work with my real estate agent. I buy houses—some for
264 re-sale as investments— "spec" houses, you know—not to live in. But I've
265 also been in the market for a vacation home for some time. At any rate, my
266 loan officer at Texas National likes Ms. Ambrose a lot and my agent knows
267 her well. So I insisted that we use Robinson and Porter to close the sale and
268 the loan. The sellers had actually wanted to hire somebody else to draw up
269 the deed, but I convinced them to let Ms. Ambrose do it. I even paid all their
270 attorney's fees so that they would let her handle the whole transaction.
271 I met with her on a couple of occasions, because the house I bought had
272 some restrictions on ownership—and disclosures about the flood plane,
273 which are rather involved—and some environmental things. We also talked
274 about her representing me in future sales of my properties.
275

276 MS. CONRAD: So on how many occasions did you meet or talk?
277

278 MR. MORGAN: Before the actual sale? I don't know—several—three or
279 four on the phone—and once in the office before the closing itself, when my
280 wife and I went up to Victoria. I talked to her once afterwards, too, about
281 some outstanding documents I hadn't yet received. There were some things
282 related to the homeowner's association—an amendment to the rules that
283 they were considering—that I wanted news about. I'd always bought and
284 sold stand-alone houses before, but the Lake Texana home is a townhouse
285 condominium, subject to restrictions on how often a home can be rented to
286 vacationers. Apparently, there've been some abuses of that rule, and they
287 were considering making the use more limited. So that was on my mind.
288 That was what started all this, in fact. That was how I came to realize she'd
289 left Robinson and Porter and was working for Mr. Hopkins.
290

291 MS. CONRAD: What do you mean?
292

293 MR. MORGAN: Well, in September—about a month or so after Architronics
294 let me go—
295

296 MR. HOPKINS: Objection. He can't characterize it as that—
297
298 MS. CONRAD: That's his view of things. It's at issue. Everyone understands
299 that.
300
301 MR. HOPKINS: I want my objection noted, your Honor.
302
303 THE COURT: So noted. Proceed.
304
305 MR. MORGAN: Okay. Well, after I was no longer at Architronics, in
306 September, I called Robinson and Porter to find out where those new
307 association rules were—because they could potentially impact the property's
308 use—so I called. But when I finally got in touch with someone, they said
309 that Ms. Ambrose was no longer there, that she'd gone in with a law firm,
310 Hopkins, Eliot and Jones. Of course, that was the second big shock in so
311 many months. I wondered if I'd heard right, and asked if it was the Hopkins
312 firm down here in Corpus Christi, and they said it was the same firm, but
313 she was stationed in an office there in Victoria, with a closing attorney. She
314 was their closing paralegal now. I hung up immediately so I could get in
315 touch with you and—well—that's why we're here, I guess.
316
317 MS. CONRAD: Tell the court why you object to Mr. Hopkins' represen-
318 tation of the Defendant. That is, how is Ms. Ambrose's employment by the
319 Hopkins firm detrimental to your case?
320
321 MR. MORGAN: Because Ms. Ambrose knows details about my thoughts on
322 the use of that home up in Lake Texana—residential or investment use, that
323 is. And she's now working for the man who represents my former employer,
324 whom I contend offered me a job they knew I couldn't take as a means to get
325 rid of me. Of course, they say I quit my job of my own free will—that I refused
326 to take an offer of transfer to Victoria, one that was "reasonable" in their view.
327 But again, my whole point is that they offered me a job they knew very well
328 I couldn't possibly take. Now, let me be clear. I'm not saying Ms. Ambrose has
329 done or would do anything to hurt me. But it's not just her that's involved.
330 This law firm represents a client that I contend did in fact hurt me. They
331 discriminated against me on the basis of my age, and all of this is related.
332
333 MS. CONRAD: All right, thank you Mr. Morgan—that's all. Your witness.
334
335   CROSS EXAMINATION OF EDWARD JAMES MORGAN
336
337 MR. HOPKINS: Your home purchase at Lake Texana is a matter of public
338 record, isn't it Mr. Morgan?
339
340 MR. MORGAN: What do you mean?
341
342 MR. HOPKINS: I mean the deed, the transfer, the documents encumber
343 ing the way that the property can be used, etc. —all of that is on record in
344 the public offices of the county, isn't it?
345

346   MR. MORGAN: Well, yes. I suppose so.

347

348   MR. HOPKINS: So anyone that wanted to find this out could do so—in fact,
349   could have done so beginning last summer, isn't that true?

350

351   MR. MORGAN: I don't know when they filed those things. But you could
352   ask your employee, Ms. Ambrose, if you're interested. She was in charge of
353   that.

354

355   MR. HOPKINS: And isn't it true that no one at Architronics knew of your
356   home purchase there?

357

358   MR. MORGAN: I don't know what they knew.

359

360   MR. HOPKINS: You never told them about it did you?

361

362   MR. MORGAN: Elizabeth knew. My colleague, Elizabeth Allen, I mean.
363   And my administrative assistant knew. Harris McKenna. I told them about
364   my business up in Victoria around the time of the closing. There might
365   have been some others. I don't recall.

366

367   MR. HOPKINS: But you never told Henry Baker, the president of
368   Architronics, or any of the upper level management with decision-making
369   authority about your home purchase, did you?

370

371   MR. MORGAN: No. I don't even see why I would.

372

373   MR. HOPKINS: But just to be clear on the timing of all this. You bought
374   the home in July of YR-1, right? What date exactly was the closing?

375

376   MR. MORGAN: July 8th.

377

378   MR. HOPKINS: And your meeting with Mr. Baker, when he made the offer
379   for you to go to the Victoria office, which you characterize as a sham offer,
380   was on August 2, YR-1, isn't that so?

381

382   MR. MORGAN: Yes.

383

384   MR. HOPKINS: So between July 8th and August 2nd, neither Mr. Baker
385   nor anyone with decision-making authority at Architronics knew about
386   your home purchase?

387

388   MR. MORGAN: I don't know what they knew.

389

390   MR. HOPKINS: You didn't tell them, though. You admitted that.

391

392   MS. CONRAD: Your Honor, there's no need for him to continue to ask
393   questions that have been answered.

394

395 MR. HOPKINS: I'm trying to place Mr. Morgan's answers within a
396 timeframe for clarity, your Honor.
397
398 THE COURT: Overruled. Answer that.
399
400 MR. MORGAN: No, I didn't tell them.
401
402 MR. HOPKINS: You said that you found out about Ms. Ambrose's current
403 employment with our firm in September. Precisely when?
404
405 MR. MORGAN: I—it was late September—around the latter part of the
406 month. Let me check my notes—is that all right?
407
408 THE COURT: Yes.
409
410 MR. MORGAN: Okay. I see. It was September 23.
411
412 MR. HOPKINS: That was after you gave sworn testimony in a deposition
413 related to your age discrimination suit, wasn't it?
414
415 MR. MORGAN: Yes.
416
417 MR. HOPKINS: You gave that deposition on September 15, YR-1. You
418 recall that?
419
420 MR. MORGAN: Yes. You deposed me yourself.
421
422 MR. HOPKINS: But in that deposition, you at no time stated anything
423 about this purchase, did you?
424
425 MR. MORGAN: I don't know what you mean.
426
427 MR. HOPKINS: I mean on that day, you never said the words "Lake Texana"
428 or "home purchase," did you?
429
430 MS. CONRAD: Your Honor, the tone of this interrogation—
431
432 MR. HOPKINS: I'll rephrase the question, your Honor, I'm sorry.
433 Mr. Morgan, in your deposition with regard to your age discrimination
434 suit, you never mentioned the purchase of this home at Lake Texana near
435 Victoria, Texas, did you?
436
437 MR. MORGAN: No. It didn't come up.
438
439 MR. HOPKINS: Why didn't it come up, though?
440
441 MR. MORGAN: I'm not a lawyer. I can't say—
442

443   MS. CONRAD: Your Honor, Mr. Morgan is not prepared to answer
444   Mr. Hopkins' quandaries about trial strategies.
445

446   THE COURT: Sustained.
447

448   MR. HOPKINS: I'll rephrase this line of questioning. Mr. Morgan. You
449   claim that the Defendant discriminated against you based upon your age,
450   isn't that correct?
451

452   MR. MORGAN: Yes.
453

454   MR. HOPKINS: Your Honor has a transcript of that deposition?
455

456   THE COURT: Yes, your office gave it to me.
457

458   MR. HOPKINS: And Mr. Morgan, in that deposition you claim that the
459   Defendant had a new computer-assisted design program—a "CAD"
460   program—that you were not allowed to learn, and in that deposition you
461   make allegations that certain comments were made about your age, and
462   in that deposition you state other matters related to your qualification for
463   the job you held there, and the lack of qualifications of your replacement,
464   don't you?
465

466   MR. MORGAN: Yes.
467

468   MR. HOPKINS: All of that is part of your age discrimination suit?
469

470   MR. MORGAN: Yes.
471

472   MR. HOPKINS: But neither you nor your counsel brought up the real
473   estate purchase in Lake Texana?
474

475   MR. MORGAN: No.
476

477   MR. HOPKINS: Because you didn't think they were related, isn't that so?
478   Isn't that why you left that information out?
479

480   MR. MORGAN: I don't know what I thought at the time. I know that I did
481   speak of the difficulties of moving or commuting to Victoria, considering
482   my circumstances.
483

484   MR. HOPKINS: When did you notify your attorney, Ms. Conrad, about
485   learning of Ms. Ambrose's new employment? How soon after September 23?
486

487   MR. MORGAN: It was that very day. She couldn't call me back—she was
488   away on business—but I left a message about all this and then we talked
489   the very next day over the phone. Then I went downtown to meet with her
490   a few days later, when she got back from her trip.
491

492 MR. HOPKINS: So you notified her September 23?

493

494 MR. MORGAN: Well, actually, we didn't get to talk until September 24.

495

496 MR. HOPKINS: So she knew of all this on September 24?

497

498 MR. MORGAN: Yes.

499

500 MR. HOPKINS: And you met in person with her on September 26?

501

502 MR. MORGAN: That's right.

503

504 MR. HOPKINS: And how did you proceed with your action, consider-
505 ing that you were so alarmed about Ms. Ambrose's new place of
506 employment?

507

508 MR. MORGAN: I don't know what you mean by that. Once I told Ms. Conrad
509 about what I'd learned of Ms. Ambrose, she said for me to hold on until she
510 got back to town. Then when we met in person, she said we should just
511 wait and see how things developed as we went along. We proceeded with
512 the lawsuit itself—with my claim, that is—in the ordinary way, I suppose.
513 She was out of town a good deal before Christmas, so I wasn't able to reach
514 her in December.

515

516 MR. HOPKINS: You tried to reach her about this matter in December—
517 I mean in particular, about Ms. Ambrose moving to our firm?

518

519 MR. MORGAN: Yes, among other things. I was just checking in. But she
520 was back east, home for Christmas I was told.

521

522 MR. HOPKINS: Your Honor, please note that this motion was not filed
523 with your court until December 30, YR-1, even taking into account the
524 major holidays and office closings in the last few months of the year.
525 I've filed an affidavit with your court stating that was also the first time
526 that I or anyone in my office was informed of the matter by Plaintiff's
527 counsel.

528

529 THE COURT: So noted.

530

531 MR. HOPKINS: And Mr. Morgan, since you learned where Ms. Ambrose
532 was working on September 23, you haven't tried to get in touch with her
533 about the information that you wanted with regard to your Lake Texana
534 home, have you?

535

536 MR. MORGAN: No. All of that got moved to the back burner, once my age
537 discrimination suit started going. Besides, I've been very busy, looking for
538 a new job and helping out with my family.

539

540 MR. HOPKINS: But the information you so urgently wanted on September
541 23, so that you took the initiative to call looking for Ms. Ambrose, you
542 have not continued to seek since you met with Ms. Conrad in person on
543 September 26th?
544
545 MR. MORGAN: I still want that information. I've just been busy with all
546 this litigation since then. I expect her to send them to me. But I had to
547 speak to my lawyer about where Ms. Ambrose was working. I didn't want
548 to create any kind of problem by getting in touch with her.
549
550 MR. HOPKINS: What kind of problem did you expect?
551
552 MR. MORGAN: Again, I'm not a lawyer. I couldn't foresee what kind of
553 error I might commit by getting in touch with your office to talk to one of
554 your employees.
555
556 MR. HOPKINS: I have no further questions of Mr. Morgan, your Honor.
557
558 THE COURT: You can step down, Mr. Morgan. Now. Ms. Conrad? Your
559 next witness.
560
561 MS. CONRAD: I'd like to call Ms. Ambrose as my final witness, your Honor. But
562 if Mr. Hopkins intends to call her, I'll just cross-examine after he's finished.
563
564 THE COURT: Mr. Hopkins?
565
566 MR. HOPKINS: I do intend to call Ms. Ambrose.
567
568 THE COURT: Then you can do that now. Is she your only witness, too?
569
570 MR. HOPKINS: Yes.
571
572 THE COURT: All right. Then Ms. Ambrose on direct from Mr. Hopkins,
573 then on cross from Ms. Conrad.
574
575 MR. HOPKINS: Ms. Ambrose, would you take the stand?
576
577 [Ms. Ambrose is sworn]
578
579   DIRECT EXAMINATION OF ELLEN HUTCHINS AMBROSE
580
581 MR. HOPKINS: State your name for the court please and your profession.
582
583 MS. AMBROSE: Ellen Hutchins Ambrose. I'm a paralegal.
584
585 MR. HOPKINS: You received a degree in that area?
586
587 MS. AMBROSE: Yes. From the program at San Jacinto College in Houston
588 in YR-14.
589

590 MR. HOPKINS: Recently, you came to work for our firm at what time?
591
592 MS. AMBROSE: August 25, YR-1.
593
594 MR. HOPKINS: And where is your current office?
595
596 MS. AMBROSE: It's in Victoria—not Corpus Christi. I stayed up there to
597 do real estate work in the Victoria branch of the firm. So I didn't move down
598 here when I left Robinson and Porter.
599
600 MR. HOPKINS: What kind of work do you do for our firm?
601
602 MS. AMBROSE: Real estate work, exclusively. In particular, I close
603 residential real estate loans, purchases and financing.
604
605 MR. HOPKINS: You do no other type of work? No litigation work?
606
607 MS. AMBROSE: None.
608
609 MR. HOPKINS: Before that, how did you come to work on Mr. Morgan's
610 home purchase while you were with Robinson and Porter?
611
612 MS. AMBROSE: I closed the home purchase loan from Texas National
613 Bank to Mr. Morgan. I did all the closing work for that bank. I continue to
614 do so now that I'm with the Hopkins firm.
615
616 MR. HOPKINS: Now, you represented the Bank's loan to Mr. Morgan to
617 purchase the home, closed the loan for the bank, received the title, and
618 wrote the title insurance policy for Mr. Morgan, correct?
619
620 MS. AMBROSE: Yes.
621
622 MR. HOPKINS: And the title insurance policy for the Bank?
623
624 MS. AMBROSE: Yes.
625
626 MR. HOPKINS: Could you relate for the court how our firm came to realize
627 that you had closed Mr. Morgan's house loan?
628
629 MS. AMBROSE: All right. On December 14 of last year, I was down at the
630 Corpus Christi office. I come down once a month to meet with you or one
631 of the other senior partners, to apprise you of how things are going. And
632 as soon as I walked in, you asked me about an envelope that you'd received
633 two days before.
634
635 MR. HOPKINS: What envelope was that?
636

637 MS. AMBROSE: It was an overnight envelope, one of those plastic bags, that
638 was addressed to me, forwarded to your office from my old office at Robinson
639 and Porter. It was sent to me in care of you. I don't know why they sent
640 it to the Corpus Christi branch. I'd left my forwarding address with them
641 and they knew I was in Victoria, but someone there—maybe a temp—who
642 knows—just forwarded it to Hopkins, Eliot, and Jones in Corpus Christi.
643
644 MR. HOPKINS: When we met on December 14, what was said to you about
645 the envelope?
646
647 MS. AMBROSE: You said your secretary, Madeleine, who opens your mail,
648 had opened the envelope two days before and was confused about it. It just
649 contained some documents and a cover letter to me concerning the matter of
650 "Edward Morgan's Lake Texana Home." She gave the documents to you. You
651 said you recognized the name in the "Re" line, immediately put them back
652 in the envelope and set them aside. You had to go to trial that afternoon and
653 would have to be there all day the next day as well. So you asked Madeleine to
654 call me about it. She had my number on her cell phone—we're good friends.
655
656 MR. HOPKINS: Was she able to reach you that afternoon of December
657 12th?
658
659 MS. AMBROSE: No. I was out for a few days, on vacation, but I was to come
660 by your office in Corpus Christi on the morning of the 14th anyway, for our
661 usual meeting.
662
663 MR. HOPKINS: And what did I say to you on the 14th about this matter
664 in particular.
665
666 MS. AMBROSE: You asked me straight off what the documents meant.
667 I had to think for a moment, and then I said something like "Oh, I closed a
668 loan the bank made to him last summer."
669
670 MR. HOPKINS: You had no idea of any potential significance of that closing
671 to Mr. Morgan's age discrimination suit when you saw the documents?
672
673 MS. AMBROSE: No. How could I? I close hundreds of loans a year.
674 I underwent a conflicts check upon re-joining the firm, and was asked to
675 disclose all of my former and current clients. I did so, and of course they were
676 all the institutional lenders that had retained me to close their loans—banks,
677 of course, and building and loans, that kind of thing. They've always been my
678 clients, and I informed the firm as much when asked who all I'd represented.
679 I certainly knew nothing about Mr. Morgan's troubles with his employer.
680
681 MR. HOPKINS: What happened then, on the 14th I mean, after our
682 exchange regarding the documents?
683
684 MS. AMBROSE: You called Mr. Eliot into your office, along with Madeleine
685 and me, and explained that Mr. Morgan was suing your client, Architronics,

686 in an age discrimination matter. You said that from that point forward, the
687 firm was instating what's called a "Chinese Wall" around me—that I was to
688 have no access to any documents in the office, was to have no contact with
689 you or anyone who was working on the Architronics case, and was to disclose
690 nothing that was related to Mr. Morgan's home purchase at Lake Texana.
691
692 MR. HOPKINS: Your Honor is in possession of an affidavit signed by those
693 parties attesting to what Ms. Ambrose has just said about the events of
694 that meeting?
695
696 THE COURT: Yes.
697
698 MR. HOPKINS: Ms. Ambrose, have you abided by our agreement at all
699 times since that day, and up to and including the present day?
700
701 MS. AMBROSE: Yes. At all times, up to and including today.
702
703 MR. HOPKINS: And who in our law firm knows anything at all about
704 Mr. Morgan's home purchase besides you?
705
706 MS. AMBROSE: No one.
707
708 MR. HOPKINS: No further questions, your Honor. Your witness, Ms. Conrad.
709
710   CROSS EXAMINATION OF ELLEN HUTCHINS AMBROSE
711
712 MS. CONRAD: Now, Ms. Ambrose, you say you came to work for
713 Mr. Hopkins in August of this last year, am I right?
714
715 MS. AMBROSE: Yes.
716
717 MS. CONRAD: And why did you do that?
718
719 MS. AMBROSE: Well, they made me a very good offer. I'd received several
720 around that time, and theirs was the best.
721
722 MS. CONRAD: You were looking for better work?
723
724 MS. AMBROSE: No, but I had just received several offers. I've been very
725 fortunate in the field. I've gotten a good reputation for efficiency and hard
726 work and just all-around productivity. People get to know you from all
727 of the deals that you close. So I had several firms—law firms and title
728 companies—that were interested in hiring me.
729
730 MS. CONRAD: So, just to be clear, you could've accepted any one of several
731 jobs, but chose to go with Hopkins, Eliot, and Jones?
732
733 MS. AMBROSE: Yes.
734

735 MS. CONRAD: But you've known Mr. Hopkins longer, haven't you?
736
737 MS. AMBROSE: Yes.
738
739 MS. CONRAD: How long?
740
741 MS. AMBROSE: About two years.
742
743 MS. CONRAD: You worked for Mr. Hopkins before your current employment,
744 though, isn't that true?
745
746 MS. AMBROSE: Yes. I was at the firm—
747
748 MS. CONRAD: Hopkins, Eliot, and Jones, you mean?
749
750 MS. AMBROSE: Yes, with them for about ten months, starting in January,
751 YR-2. Before that I worked as a closing agent for an escrow company here
752 in town.
753
754 MS. CONRAD: What kind of paralegal work did you do for the firm when
755 you first worked there?
756
757 MS. AMBROSE: General work. All kinds of business work and a little
758 litigation. But then I started to do more and more real estate work. That's
759 my preference and what I do exclusively now, as I said. I wouldn't know
760 how to do anything else at this point.
761
762 MS. CONRAD: So you left the firm in—
763
764 MS. AMBROSE: Around the end of September, YR-2.
765
766 MS. CONRAD: You went to work for Robinson and Porter up in Victoria at
767 that time?
768
769 MS. AMBROSE: Yes, they made me an offer to head up their offices there
770 and I accepted it. Reluctantly, since I had good friends at Hopkins. But I
771 couldn't turn down the opportunity at the time.
772
773 MS. CONRAD: Who are your good friends there?
774
775 MS. AMBROSE: Well, lots of people. Mr. Hopkins' assistant, Madeleine
776 Cason, is an old friend from college. And several other folks.
777
778 MS. CONRAD: How big is Hopkins, Eliot, and Jones?
779
780 MS. AMBROSE: The Corpus Christi office? Or including the satellite offices?
781
782 MS. CONRAD: How many are in each?
783

784 MS. AMBROSE: Well, I'd have to think about it. In the main office here
785 in town, there are—fifteen attorneys. Then there are five in the office in
786 Beaumont, and then in my little office in Victoria, which was only opened
787 last year, there's just one attorney and me. We do the residential real
788 estate work—a lot of vacation homes are in that area, being so close to the
789 Gulf and the Lake District. Of course, you'd have to confirm this with
790 Mr. Hopkins. I think that number's right.
791
792 THE COURT: Is that the right number, Mr. Hopkins, in each office?
793
794 MR. HOPKINS: Yes.
795
796 MS. CONRAD: Why did you come back to work for Mr. Hopkins?
797
798 MR. HOPKINS: Objection your Honor. That's a mischaracterization. She
799 doesn't work "for me." We just established that I do exclusively litigation
800 work and she's a real estate closing paralegal in another branch.
801
802 MS. CONRAD: Mr. Hopkins is a senior partner in the firm, your Honor.
803 I don't see why it's a mischaracterization to say Ms. Ambrose works "for
804 him."
805
806 THE COURT: There's no harm in putting it that way. Overruled.
807
808 MS. CONRAD: So why did you come back to the firm?
809
810 MS. AMBROSE: They were setting up a satellite office there with Virginia—
811 that's the attorney I work with, Virginia Latham—and they wanted to take
812 advantage of the business in the area, so they made me a good offer and
813 I accepted it.
814
815 MS. CONRAD: You've had more than a purely professional relationship
816 with Mr. Hopkins though, isn't that right?
817
818 MS. AMBROSE: Well, we went out some last summer, before I started
819 working for the firm again. Only a few times. Dinner and a party once.
820 Very casual and friendly. We haven't been out since then, except for lunch a
821 few times—and those were just business lunches really. At any rate, those
822 lunches were before all this stuff with Mr. Morgan started.
823
824 MS. CONRAD: Why were you having business lunches with Mr. Hopkins if
825 you're a real estate paralegal and he's a litigator?
826
827 MS. AMBROSE: As I said, he's my boss. When I started, it was agreed that
828 I'd check into the Corpus Christi office once a month. While I'm down here,
829 we've had lunch—just so he could see how things are going with the office
830 in Victoria. But again, these lunches were before any of us had knowledge
831 that I'd closed a real estate loan for Mr. Morgan.
832

833 MS. CONRAD: I don't understand. It's part of your relationship with the
834 firm to check in once a month at the Corpus Christi office. You said that
835 just now. Is that still the case?
836

837 MS. AMBROSE: It's still the case, but now I speak with another senior
838 attorney there, Mr. John Eliot—not Mr. Hopkins—if I need to talk to a
839 partner. I don't deal with Mr. Hopkins at all.
840

841 MS. CONRAD: How many real estate paralegals are there in the firm?
842

843 MS. AMBROSE: Just me. The firm does mostly litigation work, so all of
844 the others are litigation paralegals. Virginia Latham is the attorney that
845 oversees me directly.
846

847 MS. CONRAD: Then why do you not report to her?
848

849 MS. AMBROSE: I do, but I sort of run the office too—we have a secretary
850 and a title searcher. Virginia writes opinion letters and makes legal
851 decisions. But I'm kind of the office manager as well as the closing agent,
852 so I run the office and deal with the main office in Corpus Christi, to let
853 them know how things are going. I'm new at that, and the office manager in
854 the main firm, Charlotte Davidson, helps make sure I'm doing everything
855 I need to do. That's just the way they set it up.
856

857 MS. CONRAD: But if something major comes up in your office, can Mr. Eliot
858 make a decision regarding its disposition without consulting his partners?
859

860 MS. AMBROSE: I don't know the answer to that.
861

862 MS. CONRAD: Has Mr. Hopkins visited the Victoria office since your
863 hire?
864

865 MS. AMBROSE: What do you mean?
866

867 MS. CONRAD: You said that you were not allowed to talk to Mr. Hopkins
868 as part of the wall, and only allowed in certain areas of the firm, but did
869 Mr. Hopkins ever visit your offices?
870

871 MS. AMBROSE: I—yes—once he did, as I recall—he came by for lunch
872 before all this started.
873

874 MS. CONRAD: Were you forbidden from any compensation that might
875 come from the age discrimination suit your firm was defending against?
876

877 MS. AMBROSE: No, but I'm a salaried employee. I wouldn't get those kinds
878 of benefits.
879

880 MS. CONRAD: You can get bonuses though?
881

882   MS. AMBROSE: Yes, but I'm sure they'd relate to my real estate work, not to
883   litigation work. I've never, wherever I worked, received any other kind of bonus.
884

885   MS. CONRAD: But let me restate the question, you weren't forbidden from
886   compensation from this suit expressly?
887

888   MS. AMBROSE: No, I wasn't.
889

890   MS. CONRAD: You weren't physically separated from the main firm
891   either—that is, told not to go to the offices?
892

893   MS. AMBROSE: Well, I think it's obvious that I am in fact physically
894   separated from the offices—every day. I'm in another building, in another
895   town, an hour and a half away.
896

897   MS. CONRAD: But you could come to the office in Corpus Christi, though.
898   That wasn't forbidden to you, was it?
899

900   MS. AMBROSE: Like I said. I run that office up there. I'm required to come
901   by once a month. I meet only with the office manager and Mr. Eliot, if need
902   be, and say hello to my friends. But that's all.
903

904   MS. CONRAD: You haven't completely finished with the house purchase
905   relating to Mr. Morgan, have you?
906

907   MS. AMBROSE: Yes, I have. All but forwarding an amended set of Home
908   Owner's Restrictions for Lakeview, the development he's a part of. But
909   that's all I have to do. The group's been hard to get hold of and the proposed
910   amendment hadn't been adopted when last I spoke to the Home Owner's
911   Association President back in early August.
912

913   MS. CONRAD: The Home Owner's Restrictions relate to the use of the
914   property—that is, how it can be used, for sale, recreation, etc.?
915

916   MS. AMBROSE: They do, among other things, but the amendment relates
917   to how often the property can be rented for vacation purposes. That's the
918   controversy they're settling, the Lake View homeowners that is. Anyhow,
919   I was just going to forward those to Mr. Morgan when they settled the
920   point. I was the contact person for him in the area and had forwarded
921   everything else associated with the closing to him down in Kingsville. It's
922   a formality. A business practice—good service, that's all. The significance of
923   the restrictions to Mr. Morgan is something he'd have to speak to himself.
924

925   MS. CONRAD: But you do have a current set of restrictions with you at the
926   firm, in a file dedicated to his business, right?
927

928   MS. AMBROSE: I have a current set of restrictions in a file, and a draft
929   of the amendment. There might be some notes on the documents about

930 Mr. Morgan's closing, but that's all. Once I get the final amended
931 restrictions, I'll forward the entire thing to him.
932

933 MS. CONRAD: Now, Ms. Ambrose, by closing the loan and writing the
934 title insurance policy, you were making sure that both the Bank and
935 Mr. Morgan were receiving good, insurable title, weren't you? I mean, his
936 interest and the Bank's interest were one, which is usually the case in
937 loans and purchases, correct?
938

939 MS. AMBROSE: They tend to be, yes, as a matter of course.
940

941 MS. CONRAD: And you and the lawyer that supervised you were in charge
942 of the interests of Texas National Bank and Mr. Morgan.
943

944 MS. AMBROSE: The Bank hired us though.
945

946 MS. CONRAD: But the loan closing fee was paid by Mr. Morgan, as part of
947 the loan proceeds, wasn't it? Isn't that typical and wasn't that the case here?
948

949 MS. AMBROSE: Yes, that's the case.
950

951 MS. CONRAD: And he also paid your fee for preparing the sale documents
952 for the seller?
953

954 MS. AMBROSE: Yes, but I never told him that I was representing him.
955

956 MS. CONRAD: You knew that he insisted, as he's testified, on your closing
957 the entire transaction, and that he also understood you to be representing
958 his interests?
959

960 MS. AMBROSE: Well, I suppose. He did seem to be under that impression.
961

962 MS. CONRAD: And upon discovering this potential conflict, to your
963 knowledge, your office did not notify Mr. Morgan about it, did you?
964

965 MS. AMBROSE: Well, no. But there were only two weeks between our being
966 surprised by this knowledge and your filing this motion—and this was all
967 during the Christmas holidays, too.
968

969 MS. CONRAD: Why didn't you notify him? You had the ability, didn't you?
970

971 MS. AMBROSE: In that short time, the most important thing was for us to
972 set up the screen around me and to comply with Texas law on this matter.
973 In my opinion, notifying Mr. Morgan was preempted by the speed of this
974 motion—something that could only occur because the two of you had known
975 about this a lot longer than we had.
976

977 MS. CONRAD: That's all I have your Honor.
978

979 THE COURT: If that's it for both sides, you can step down Ms. Ambrose.
980 Thank you.
981
982 MR. HOPKINS: Your Honor? One more thing. I'd like to submit for your
983 consideration the following documents: the docket sheet regarding this
984 matter, which relates to timing; the restrictions regarding the real property
985 in Victoria; and my bio from our firm's website. I have copies for Ms. Conrad
986 as well.
987
988 THE COURT: All right. Thank you.
989
990 [end of proceedings at 11:00 a.m. C.S.T.]
991
992
993
994   C E R T I F I C A T E
995
996 I certify that the foregoing is a correct transcript from the record of
997 proceedings in the above-entitled matter, to the best of my ability.
998
999 *McKenzie Smith*
1000 McKenzie Smith, CSR, RDR, CRR   January 5, YEAR

U.S. District Court
SOUTHERN DISTRICT OF TEXAS (Corpus Christi)
CIVIL DOCKET FOR CASE # 12345

Morgan v. Architronics, Inc.
Date Filed: 08/18/YR-1
Date Terminated:
Jury Demand: Plaintiff
Nature of Suit: 440 Other Civil Rights
Jurisdiction: Federal Question

Edward G. Morgan   represented by Rebecca A. Conrad
Conrad & Conrad, LLP
Suite 1056, Commerce Place
Corpus Christi, Texas 78470
316-555-2134
Fax: 316-555-1211
conrad@conrad.com

Architronics, Inc.   represented by G. Mark Hopkins
Hopkins, Eliot, and Jones
Attorneys at Law
567 Harrison Place South
Corpus Christi, Texas 78470
316-555-4312
Fax: 316-555-2111
heijlawfirm.com

Date Filed	#	Docket Text
08/18/YR-1	1	COMPLAINT by Edward J. Morgan (Entered: 08/18/YR-1)
09/02/YR-1	2	ANSWER by Architronics, Inc. (Entered 09/02/YR-1)
09/05/YR-1	3	SCHEDULING ORDER (Entered 09/05/YR-1) (setting discovery cut-off of 01/30/YEAR & trial date of 02/23/YEAR)
09/09/YR-1	4	INTERROGATORY REQUEST (Morgan)
09/10/YR-1	5	INTERROGATORY REQUEST (Architronics)

09/15/ YR-1	6	DEP. EDWARD J. MORGAN (by G. Mark Hopkins)
09/29/YR-1	7	DEP. ELIZABETH ALLEN (by Rebecca Conrad)
10/18/YR-1	8	DEP. MARGARET ELLISON (by Rebecca Conrad)
12/01/YR-1	9	DEP. HENRY BAKER (by Rebecca Conrad) AFF. PHILIP WHITLOW
12/05/YR-1	10	DEP. STEPHEN ABERNATHY (by Rebecca Conrad)
12/30/YR-1	11	MOT. TO DISQUALIFY COUNSEL
01/02/YEAR	12	OPP. TO MOT. TO DISQUALIFY COUNSEL
01/05/YEAR	13	TR. OF HEARING ON MOT. TO DISQUALIFY

DECLARATION OF COVENANTS, CONDITIONS, AND RESTRICTIONS

LAKEVIEW HOMEOWNER'S ASSOCIATION RULES AND REGULATIONS

THIS DECLARATION, made this 5th day of June, YR-3, by Lakeview Development Co., Inc., a Texas corporation, which has offices at 128 Belle Rive Drive, Victoria, Texas, being hereinafter referred to as the "Developer."

....

ARTICLE IV.

In addition to all of the covenants and conditions contained in this declaration of townhouse condominium, the use of the property and each condominium is subject to the following:

SECTION ONE. USE AND OCCUPANCY

A.   Without the prior written consent of the Lakeview Board of Directors, no unit shall be occupied and used except for residential purposes by the owner or owners, his or her or their tenants, and social guests, and no trade or business shall be conducted in the condominium, except a residential unit may be used as a combined residence and executive or professional office by the owner or owners of the unit, so long as such use does not interfere with the quiet enjoyment by other residential unit owners of their units. No tent, shack, trailer, basement, garage, outbuilding, or structure of a temporary character shall be used at any time as a residence, either temporarily or permanently.

B.   Residents shall be limited as follows:

....

4.   No unit or any portion of a unit in the project shall be leased, subleased, occupied, rented, let, sublet, or used for or in connection with any time-sharing agreement, plan, program, or arrangement, including, but not limited to, any so-called "vacation license," "travel club," "extended vacation," or other membership or time-interval ownership arrangement, for more than fifty-six (56) days per year. The term "time-sharing" as used in this provision shall be deemed to include, but shall not be limited to, any agreement, plan, program, or arrangement under which the right to use, occupy, or possess the unit or any of the unit in the project rotates among various persons, either corporate, partnership, individual, or otherwise, on a periodically recurring basis for value exchanged, whether monetary or like-kind use privileges, according to a fixed or floating interval or period of time of seven *[7]* consecutive calendar days or less. These provisions shall not be construed, however, to limit the personal use of any unit or any portion of such unit in the project by any unit owner or owners or his or her or their social or familial guests.

....

DEED BOOK <u>2678</u> PAGE <u>567</u>, County Clerk's Office, Jackson County, Texas.

(from: www.hejlawfirm.com/attorneyprofiles)

HOPKINS, ELIOT, and JONES
ATTORNEYS AT LAW

G. Mark Hopkins, Managing Partner

JD, University of Texas
Bar Admissions: Texas; Oklahoma; Federal Trial Bar

Practice Focus

A respected labor and employment attorney, G. Mark Hopkins has more than 25 years of experience in those areas, advising businesses on compliance with labor and employment laws. He has served as outside counsel to various corporations in fields as diverse as architecture, aviation, and oil and gas. Mr. Hopkins has been admitted to the Federal Trial Bar, and has argued cases before both federal and state courts. He has been formally recognized by his peers as one of the leading lawyers in the area of labor and employment law, receiving an AV® rating from the Martindale-Hubbell Review Ratings. He has chaired several state advisory committees in that area, and has served as a Visiting Lecturer in Employment Law at St. Mary's University Law School in San Antonio, Texas. He has published over twenty articles in various law journals and trade publications on labor and employment law.

ORAL DEFENSE OF MOTION
TO DISQUALIFY BRIEF

Conrad & Conrad, LLP
Suite 1056, Commerce Place
Corpus Christi, Texas 78470
Telephone: 316-555-2134
Facsimile: 316-555-1211
conrad@conrad.com

INTEROFFICE MEMORANDUM

From: Rebecca A. Conrad
To: Associate Attorney
Re: Motion to Disqualify G. Mark Hopkins
Date: Today, YEAR.

Prepare an oral argument of the motion's brief written with regard to the above-referenced matter. The argument will be held in the federal court of the Southern District of Texas. The judge will allot the time limits and the argument protocols set out in the attachment to this letter.

Rac/bb

Hopkins, Eliot, and Jones
Attorneys at Law
567 Harrison Place South
Corpus Christi, Texas 78470
Telephone: 316-555-4312
Facsimile: 316-555-2111
hejlawfirm.com

INTEROFFICE MEMORANDUM

From: G. Mark Hopkins
To: Associate Attorney
Re: Motion to Disqualify G. Mark Hopkins
Date: Today, YEAR.

Prepare an oral argument of the motion's brief written with regard to the above-referenced matter. The argument will be held in the federal court of the Southern District of Texas. The judge will allot the time limits and the argument protocols set out in the attachment to this letter.

GMH: mc

APPELLATE BRIEF: MOTION TO DISQUALIFY

Conrad & Conrad, LLP
Suite 1056, Commerce Place
Corpus Christi, Texas 78470
Telephone: 316-555-2134
Facsimile: 316-555-1211
conrad@conrad.com

INTEROFFICE MEMORANDUM

From: Rebecca A. Conrad
To: Associate Attorney
Re: Motion to Disqualify
Date: Today, YEAR.

As you know, M. Leigh Barksdale has handed down his order with regard to the above-referenced matter. Appeals/Cross appeals have been requested and granted. The order and all appellate documents are attached.
Review these materials and draft an appellate brief to the Fifth Circuit.

Rac/bb

Hopkins, Eliot, and Jones
Attorneys at Law
567 Harrison Place South
Corpus Christi, Texas 78470
Telephone: 316-555-4312
Facsimile: 316-555-2111
hejlawfirm.com

INTEROFFICE MEMORANDUM

From: G. Mark Hopkins
To: Associate Attorney
Re: Motion to Disqualify
Date: Today, YEAR.

As you know, M. Leigh Barksdale has handed down his order with regard to the above-referenced matter. Appeals/Cross appeals have been requested and granted. The order and all appellate documents are attached. Review these materials and draft an appellate brief to the Fifth Circuit.

GMH: mc

Assignment 13

MEDIATION

UNITED STATES COURT OF APPEALS
FOR THE FIFTH CIRCUIT
600 Camp Street
New Orleans, LA 20130

505-555-0987

OFFICE OF THE APPELLATE CONFERENCE PROGRAM

March 15, YEAR

Via Electronic and U.S. Mail

Rebecca Conrad, Esq.
Conrad & Conrad, LLP
Suite 1056, Commerce Place
Corpus Christi, TX 78470

G. Mark Hopkins, Esq.
Hopkins, Eliot, & Jones
567 Harrison Place South
Corpus Christi, TX 78470

Re: Morgan v. Architronics, Inc., No. 09-1099

Dear Counsel:

The Office of the Appellate Conference Program has selected this appeal for inclusion in the court's Appellate Conference Program. The mediator assigned to your case is:

Page Brent, Esq.
600 Camp Street
New Orleans, LA 20130
pbrent@acplaw.net

A copy of the mediator's biography is enclosed. If you have any concerns about the impartiality of the assigned mediator, including any bias that might be perceived by others, please email the Appellate Conference Program Attorney's Office at the address listed above immediately. Describe any and all past relationships the assigned mediator has had with counsel, counsel's firm or the parties, and any conflicts you believe the assigned mediator might have.

Assuming no conflict exists, **please contact the above-referenced mediator within five days of the date of this letter** to discuss the logistics of conference. To familiarize yourself with the general guidelines of the conference process, you are asked to review the enclosed "General Order Governing the Appellate Conference Program" ("Order").

The enclosed Order explains the confidentiality responsibilities of the mediator. Each party, party representative, attorney and person, party or attorney assisting them also must maintain confidentiality with respect to any settlement communications made or received during or incident to the mediation process.

Each party is to be represented at the mediation by its principal attorney and by a party representative with actual settlement authority.

Do not hesitate to contact me directly at 505-555-0987 if I may be of further assistance. I wish you success in your conference.

Sincerely,

Millicent LaVesque

Millicent LaVesque
Assistant Appellate Conference Attorney

MRJ:nbb

Enc.:   Order
cc: Page Brent, Esq.

1.   What usually happens at the initial conference?

The primary purpose of the initial conference is evaluation of whether the case is a good candidate for further settlement discussions. There may be some discussion of the legal issues and the underlying facts, but the conference is not a dress rehearsal for oral argument. The attorneys should expect to be asked about their client's general attitude toward settlement of the case, but normally will not be asked to have specific settlement authority for the initial conference.

2.   Is the client or client representative allowed to participate?

Yes, although their participation is not necessary for the initial conference. If you want a client representative (or another attorney) added to the conference call, let us know in advance of the conference.

3.   How long does the initial conference last?

Generally between 15 and 45 minutes, but very rarely longer than one hour.

4.   What should be in the issue statement?

The issue statement is meant to briefly inform the conference attorney of what issues will be raised on appeal. It should not contain extended argument, but should be more specific than "The district court erred in granting summary judgment." When the district court did not write an opinion, or wrote one that does not address the underlying facts, it is helpful if the issue statement also provides information about the factual background of the case.

5.   I don't think the case is likely to settle. Should I opt out of the program?

That depends. If your conclusion is based on what you know about your client's interests and intentions, then you probably should opt out. If your client would be willing to talk about settlement but believes that the other side will be unreasonable, our advice is generally not to opt out -- sometimes, having a neutral third party ask questions of your opposing counsel yields surprising results.

6.   What if I'm not available at the stated date and time for the conference?

You can call us to reschedule. It is much easier if you call opposing counsel first and supply us with a few alternative times and dates when both sides are available.

GENERAL ORDER GOVERNING THE APPELLATE CONFERENCE PROGRAM
EFFECTIVE MARCH 27, 2000

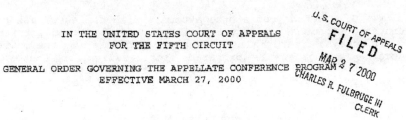

O R D E R:

1.   Pursuant to Federal Rules of Appellate Procedure Rule 33, it is hereby ORDERED that, in matters selected for participation in the court's appellate conference program, or referred to the program by the court, conference proceedings shall be conducted in accordance with the provisions of this General Order.

2.   Counsel will be notified by letter of the date and time scheduled for the initial conference. Conferences may be conducted by telephone or in person at the option of the conference attorney or upon request of all parties. Conferences will be scheduled and adjourned at the conference attorney's discretion, with due regard for the availability and convenience of counsel.

3.   The principal purpose of the conference program is to explore the possibility of settlement and to facilitate settlement discussions.   Conferences may also entail consideration of simplification, clarification, and reduction of issues, and any other matters relating to the efficient management and disposition of the appeal.

4.   Counsel's participation is required at any scheduled conference. The conference attorney may also require attendance by the parties in person or through appropriate corporate representatives or representatives of insurers providing a defense. After a case has been assigned to the conference program, any party may submit to the conference attorney a written request not to participate in or to terminate settlement discussions. In cases selected for the conference program by the conference attorney, such a request will be honored, and any further conference proceedings will be restricted to the other purposes of the conference program. In cases referred to the conference program by the court, the request will be submitted to the court, and conference proceedings will be held in abeyance pending further directions from the court.

5.   The conference attorney may require counsel to provide pertinent written information or materials, including position statements, lists of issues, outlines of arguments or other documents that the conference attorney believes may be helpful in accomplishing the purposes of conferences under Rule 33.

6.   During the pendency of conference proceedings, counsel

should provide the conference attorney with copies of all filings and correspondence sent to the clerk. Counsel should not send the clerk copies of materials or documents requested by the conference attorney or otherwise prepared specifically for the program. Documents created for the program and furnished to the conference attorney will not be included in the court's file.

7.   The time allowed for filing of briefs will not be tolled automatically by proceedings pursuant to this order. If the parties are engaged in settlement discussions, the conference attorney may recommend a resetting of the briefing schedule. The conference attorney may also recommend the entry of other orders controlling the course of proceedings, including orders altering the page and type-volume limitations for briefs and record excerpts.

8.   All statements made by the parties or their counsel in the course of proceedings pursuant to this order, and all documents specifically prepared for use in such proceedings, shall be without prejudice, and, apart from any settlement agreement reached, shall not be binding on the parties. Such statements and documents shall not be quoted, cited, referred to or otherwise used by the parties or their counsel in the course of the appeal or in any other proceeding, except as they may be admissible in a proceeding to enforce a settlement agreement. Such statements and documents shall be privileged from discovery by the parties except in such a proceeding.

9.   Confidentiality is required with respect to all settlement discussions conducted under conference program auspices. Information concerning such discussions shall neither be made known to the court nor voluntarily disclosed to anyone not involved in conference proceedings (or entitled to be kept informed of such proceedings), by either the conference attorney, the parties or their counsel, except insofar as such information may be admissible in a proceeding to enforce a settlement agreement and except as provided below.

10. Information about the assignment of particular cases to the program shall not be made public either by the staff of the conference program or by the clerk. For good cause (and in the absence of an explicit agreement to the contrary) the fact that a case has been assigned to the conference program may be disclosed by any party as long as substantive information about settlement discussions is not revealed, and the disclosure is not purposely used in an effort to gain an advantage over another party. Any such improper disclosure will result in the release of the case from the program. The identity of cases assigned to the program may in any event be provided to the court in statistical reports, in response to inquiries and in connection with recommendations about procedural orders.

11. Once all briefs have been filed, or when a motion is under submission to the court, the conference attorney may report to the court whether active settlement discussions are under way in order to assist the court in scheduling. Such reports may include information about the likelihood and timing of settlement, but information about the parties respective positions or other substantive aspects of settlement discussions will not be revealed to the court except upon the joint request of all parties.

12. The confidentiality provisions of this order shall extend to discussions occurring in the course of preliminary contacts between the conference attorney and counsel about the possibility of settlement, whether or not the case is eventually assigned to the program. These provisions shall also be binding on non-parties (such as insurers or parties to related disputes) who accept invitations to participate in conference proceedings. For the purposes of this order these participants shall be treated as parties, and participation in settlement discussions under the auspices of the conference program shall be deemed to constitute an agreement to be bound by the confidentiality provisions of this order.

13. Counsel for each party shall be responsible for providing a copy of this order to all persons participating in conference proceedings on behalf of that party. In addition, before disclosing any information about settlement discussions conducted under conference program auspices to any other person whose position or relationship with a party requires such disclosure, counsel shall provide such person with a copy of this order and obtain such person's agreement to be bound as a party would be bound by its provisions requiring confidentiality.

14. If a party is subject to obligations of disclosure to the public or to persons from whom such agreement cannot be obtained, counsel shall inform the conference attorney and counsel for the other party or parties. Settlement discussions may then be conducted under program auspices only if all parties agree to proceed. This order is not intended of its own force to prevent disclosure required by applicable law, but parties subject to such requirements must make every effort to maintain, to the extent permitted by such provisions of law, the confidentiality of such settlement discussions.

15. The confidentiality of any settlement agreement will be governed by the terms of that agreement and the law otherwise applicable thereto.

16. This General Order supersedes the prior General Order issued November 16, 1996, which shall nevertheless continue to be effective for cases assigned to the conference program before the date hereof.

                              Carolyn Dineen King
                                Chief Judge

March 27, 2000

Page Brent, Esq.
Office of the Appellate Conference Program
600 Camp Street
New Orleans, LA 20130
pbrent@acplaw.net

March 20, YEAR

VIA ELECTRONIC AND U.S. MAIL

Rebecca Conrad, Esq.
Conrad & Conrad, LLP
Suite 1056, Commerce Place
Corpus Christi, TX 78470

G. Mark Hopkins, Esq.
Hopkins, Eliot, & Jones
567 Harrison Place South
Corpus Christi, TX 78470

Re: <u>Morgan v. Architronics, Inc.</u>, No. 09-1099

Dear Counsel:

The Appellate Conference Program of the U.S. Court of Appeals for the Fifth Circuit previously contacted you to let you know that your case is included in the Court's Appellate Conference Program. I will be the mediator for your case, and I look forward to working with you. If at any time during this process you have questions or concerns about the mediation, please let me know and I will be glad to help. Of course, if we fail to settle your case during this scheduled conference, I am available to continue working with you if follow-up discussions or conference sessions seem useful.

This letter serves to confirm the date, time and location for the initial scheduled conference, to give you further details about the conference itself, and to explain what you need to do in preparation.

Date: April 15, YEAR, starting at 9:30 A.M.
Location: The Fifth Circuit's Appellate Conference Room

For some of you, this may be the first time you have participated in any settlement conference, while others of you may be familiar with such programs but less familiar with the Fifth Circuit's version of the process. Therefore, please review General Order Governing the Appellate

Conference Program" ("Order") sent to you by the Office of the Appellate Conference Program.

The most important aspects of mediation that distinguish it from litigation are the parties' control over the resolution of their dispute and its confidentiality. The conference allows the parties to explore options for resolving their dispute that include but also extend beyond the legal options available in court. Procedurally, the conference program is a flexible process, consisting of a mix of joint sessions and individual caucuses in which parties can discuss the legal and non-legal issues in their dispute, candidly weigh the strengths and weaknesses of their positions, and consider possible legal and non-legal solutions. Throughout this process, confidentiality protects any information related to the case. The fact that a case is in conference is not disclosed to the Court or to the public, and the outcome of the conference is likewise confidential unless all parties agree otherwise. In addition, information that you may disclose during your individual caucuses will not be shared with the other side, except to the extent that you authorize.

Prior to our mediation, I need you to send me the following two documents:

1. A list with the full names of anyone attending the conference on your client's behalf.
2. A Confidential Conference Statement ("CCS") that responds to the issues outlined below. The CCS can be sent by paper to my address above, or via email [pbrent@acplaw.net] or fax (505-555-0988). **Do not send your CCS to the Clerk's Office.** The content of your CCS is confidential and will not be shared with any other party or with the Court.

Other than the conference itself, your preparation of the CCS is the most important element in the conference process. Preparing your CCS allows you, your client, and me to have a candid view of the factual and legal hurdles that you face, the strengths and weaknesses of both sides' cases, and possible avenues to settlement. Although there is no page limit to a CSS, it is generally 2–4 pages long, depending on the complexity of the issues; it is deliberately intended to be brief but candid and thorough. The Fifth Circuit and its mediators have found that the most useful CCSs address the following issues:

A. Please give a brief <u>factual background</u> of the case, indicating any facts that are genuinely in dispute, and why.
B. Identify <u>any cases involving the same parties</u> that are either pending or decided, in any tribunal.
C. Identify any controlling or particularly relevant <u>legal authorities</u>. If these authorities are not readily available, please enclose a copy or a link where they can be reviewed.
D. Identify any <u>jurisdictional issues</u> that have been raised by any party, and give your honest assessment of the merits of these claims.

E. Is there any <u>additional information</u> that you need (from the other side, or elsewhere) before agreeing to settle? If so, how might that information be obtained?

F. Give an honest discussion of <u>your claims and defenses</u>. Please identify the strongest and weakest parts of your case and explain — legally or otherwise — their strengths and weaknesses.

G. Give an honest discussion of <u>the strongest and weakest aspects of the other side's case</u>.

H. What, in your candid assessment, is the <u>likely outcome</u> if this case continues to the Fifth Circuit on appeal?

I. Give a brief history of any <u>prior settlement negotiations</u>, and include your candid assessment as to why the case has not settled.

J. Explain any elements that your client <u>cannot compromise</u>. Identify any interests or issues that are not directly involved in this case but that might frustrate or assist in settlement.

K. A list of <u>possible settlement terms and ideas</u>. Alongside each idea, please evaluate candidly the merits of that idea and how it might be achieved.

As you prepare for conference, do not hesitate to contact me if I can be of any assistance. I wish you success in your conference endeavor.

Sincerely,

Page Brent
Page Brent, Esq.

cc: Millicent LaVesque

Assignment 14

SETTLEMENT

Conrad & Conrad, LLP
Suite 1056, Commerce Place
Corpus Christi, Texas 78470
Telephone: 316-555-2134
Facsimile: 316-555-1211
conrad@conrad.com

INTEROFFICE MEMORANDUM

From: Rebecca A. Conrad
To: Drafting Attorney
Re: Edward Morgan Matter
Date: Today, YEAR.

As you know, we have reached an agreement with Architronics, Inc. to settle Mr. Morgan's age discrimination suit against the company. The basic terms of the agreement are reflected in the attachment to this letter.
Please draft a settlement agreement reflecting these terms, and make sure that Mr. Morgan's interests are protected accordingly. Of course, opposing counsel will want to review this document before any of the parties sign.

RAC:bb

Hopkins, Eliot, and Jones
Attorneys at Law
567 Harrison Place South
Corpus Christi, Texas 78470
Telephone: 316-555-4312
Facsimile: 316-555-2111
hejlawfirm.com

INTEROFFICE MEMORANDUM

From: G. Mark Hopkins
To: Drafting Attorney
Re: Architronics Matter
Date: Today, YEAR.

As you know, we have reached an agreement with Edward Morgan to settle his age discrimination suit against the company. The basic terms of the agreement are reflected in the attachment to this letter.
Please draft a settlement agreement reflecting these terms, and make sure that Architronics is protected from any and all future claims with regard to this matter. Pay particular attention to secure compliance with any federal requirements. Of course, opposing counsel will want to review this document before Mr. Morgan signs.

GMH: mc

Assignment 15

TRIAL PRACTICE

Conrad & Conrad, LLP
Suite 1056, Commerce Place
Corpus Christi, Texas 78470
Telephone: 316-555-2134
Facsimile: 316-555-1211
conrad@conrad.com

INTEROFFICE MEMORANDUM

From: Rebecca A. Conrad
To: Associate
Re: Edward Morgan Matter
Date: Today, YEAR.

Prepare for trial in the above-referenced matter, Edward Morgan's ADEA claim. Any of the four named witnesses may be called to prove Mr. Morgan's claim. No other witness or information other than that set out below will be allowed by the court.

1. Deposition of Edward J. Morgan
2. Deposition of Henry C. Baker
3. Deposition of Margaret Ellison
4. Affidavit of Phillip Whitlow
5. Highlights of *Quixotic 3000*

The case is being heard in federal court, in the Southern District of Texas. Notification of witnesses and general court rules as to deadlines and other matters, already provided, should be observed at all times.

Hopkins, Eliot, and Jones
Attorneys at Law
567 Harrison Place South
Corpus Christi, Texas 78470
Telephone: 316-555-4312
Facsimile: 316-555-2111
hejlawfirm.com

INTEROFFICE MEMORANDUM

From: G. Mark Hopkins
To: Associate
Re: Architronics Matter
Date: Today, YEAR.

Prepare for trial in the above-referenced matter, Architronics' defense against Edward Morgan's ADEA claim. Any of the four named witnesses may be called to rebut Mr. Morgan's claim. No other witness or information other than that set out below will be allowed by the court.

1. Deposition of Edward J. Morgan
2. Deposition of Henry C. Baker
3. Deposition of Margaret Ellison
4. Affidavit of Phillip Whitlow
5. Highlights of *Quixotic 3000*

The case is being heard in federal court, in the Southern District of Texas. Notification of witnesses and general court rules as to deadlines and other matters, already provided, should be observed at all times.